PREPARING TEACHERS FOR NATIONAL BOARD CERTIFICATION

PREPARING TEACHERS FOR NATIONAL BOARD CERTIFICATION

A Facilitator's Guide

KATHLEEN ANDERSON STEEVES
BARBARA COLE BROWNE

Foreword by Mary Hatwood Futrell

THE GUILFORD PRESS
New York   London

This publication is not a publication by, and does not represent in any manner, the National
Board for Professional Teaching Standards, Inc. (the National Board). The phrases "National
Board Certification" and "National Board Certified Teacher" are federally registered
trademarks of the National Board.

Library of Congress Cataloging-in-Publication Data
Steeves, Kathleen Anderson.
    Preparing teachers for National Board certification : a facilitator's guide / Kathleen
Anderson Steeves, Barbara Cole Browne.
        p. cm.
    Includes bibliographical references and index.
    ISBN 1-57230-542-8 (pbk.)
    1. Teachers—Certification—United States.   2. Education—Standards—United States.
  3. National Board for Professional Teaching Standards (U.S.)   I. Browne, Barbara C.
  II. Title.
LB1771 .S67 2000
371.12′0973—dc21
                                                                    00-026982

About the Authors

KATHLEEN ANDERSON STEEVES, PHD, is an associate professor in secondary history/social studies education at the Graduate School of Education and Human Development of George Washington University, Washington, DC. She is a former instructor of history, social studies, and foreign language at secondary schools in Michigan, Iowa, Ohio, and Massachusetts, and a current instructor of history and education at the college/university level in Massachusetts and Connecticut, as well as Washington, DC. Active in history standards assessment and development with professional associations and school systems, she has also been a consultant to PBS, The History Channel, the Smithsonian Institution, and the National Museum of American History. She is a reviewer of the history/social studies portfolio for the National Board for Professional Teaching Standards and National Council for the Social Studies. Her research interests center around the connections between history and education. In addition to presentations she has made about the National Board, recent publications include "Teaching Beyond the Text" (1998, *Basic Education*) and "Working Together to Strengthen History Teaching in Secondary Schools" (1998, American Historical Association, on-line).

BARBARA COLE BROWNE, EDD, is an assistant research professor in early childhood special education at the Graduate School of Education and Human Development of George Washington University, Washington, DC. Currently she is coprincipal investigator on a doctoral leadership training grant and project director on a master's-level training grant at GWU, and has previously directed the GWU grant sponsored by the Pew Charitable Trust Foundation to assist teachers seeking certification by the National Board for Professional Teaching Standards (NBPTS). She has presented extensively at conferences on NBPTS support, and is the coauthor of a number of National Board-related publications. She was an expert reviewer for NBPTS on the Exceptional Needs Certification Area Assessment. Her specialty is infancy and early childhood, and she has written in that area as well. She is coauthor of *Developmental Play Group Guide* (1995, American Psychological Corporation).

Contributing Authors

NANCY AREGLADO, MEd, NBCT, Early Childhood/Generalist, Literacy Specialist, Tenafly Public Schools, Tenafly, New Jersey

BARBARA COLE BROWNE, EDD, Assistant Research Professor, Early Childhood Special Education, Graduate School of Education and Human Development, George Washington University, Washington, DC

BETTY COSTELLO, MED, Office of Staff Development, Fairfax County Public Schools, Fairfax, Virginia

MARLENE HENRIQUES, EDD, NBCT, Early Childhood/Generalist, Kindergarten, Centreville Elementary School, Centreville, Virginia

LISA HOLM, MED, NBCT, Early Childhood/Generalist, Grade 1, Rolling Valley Elementary School, Springfield, Virginia

CAROL HORN, MED, NBCT, Early Adolescence/Generalist, Grade 5, William Halley Elementary School, Fairfax, Virginia

THOMAS JOHNSON, PHD, NBCT, Adolescence/Young Adulthood/Mathematics, Jefferson Jr. High School, Washington, DC

CONSTANCE MOSAKOWSKY, BS, NBCT, Adolescence/Young Adulthood/Mathematics, Grade 9, Minnie Howard School, Alexandria, Virginia

KATHLEEN ANDERSON STEEVES, PHD, Associate Professor, Secondary History/Social Studies Education, Graduate School of Education and Human Development, George Washington University, Washington, DC

CAROL SULTZMAN, MED, NBCT, Early Adolescence/Generalist, Grades 3–6, Crestwood Elementary School, Springfield, VA

FAYE WAGONER, MA, NBCT, Early Adolescence/English Language Arts, Grade 8, Jackson Middle School, Fairfax, Virginia

RICHARD WORMELI, MA, NBCT, Early Adolescence/Generalist, Grades 7–8, Rachel Carson Middle School, Herndon, Virginia

Foreword

In May 1987 the Carnegie Foundation issued a report, *A Nation Prepared: Teachers for the 21st Century*, which brought to the forefront the critical relationship between education, the economy, and democracy. As part of the report, the Task Force on Teaching as a Profession described the crucial function of the teacher in ensuring that we, as a nation, are prepared for the 21st century. "The focus of schooling," wrote the Task Force, "must shift from teaching to learning, from the passive acquisition of facts and routines to the active application of ideas to problems. That transition makes the role of the teacher more important, not less. . . . The key to success lies in creating a profession equal to the task" (p. 25).

Of the recommendations advocated by the Task Force, the one that has taken on a life of its own is the national certification process for teachers. The National Board for Professional Teaching Standards (NBPTS) was established in 1987 to develop a voluntary, national process for certifying teachers. The NBPTS is an independent, nonprofit, nonpartisan organization governed by a 63-member board of directors. As president of the National Education Association, I served as a member of the Task Force that wrote the report and was a member of the inaugural NBPTS. Today, over half of the directors are classroom teachers. The other directors are school administrators, school board leaders, governors and state legislators, higher education officials, teacher union leaders, and business and community leaders.

The NBPTS's mission is to establish high and rigorous standards for what accomplished teachers should know and be able to do, and to develop and operate a national, voluntary system to assess and certify teachers who meet these standards. The NBPTS is also committed to advancing related education reforms for the purpose of improving student learning in U.S. schools. The NBPTS's goal is to improve student learning by strengthening teaching.

To achieve these goals, the NBPTS has identified five core propositions that define what accomplished teachers should know and be able to demonstrate. In 1993, the NBPTS piloted its first set of standards. Today standards have been approved in 16 fields, with others planned to reach teachers in 30 fields in the next five years. For the first time, the profession finds itself responsible for defining what it means to be a professional teacher.

In 1993 the Graduate School of Education and Human Development at George Washington University (GWU) made a commitment to support teachers in the Tristate Metropolitan Area (Maryland, Virginia, and the District of Columbia) who wanted to become nationally certified. The Fairfax County Public School system in Virginia joined with GWU to develop a pilot program designed to recruit and support teachers seeking national certification. Thanks to the generous support of the Pew Charitable Trust Foundation, we have since been able to expand our outreach efforts and to work with an increasing number of school districts. Today, a number of school districts in the metropolitan area have teachers who are NBPTS certified. The number of teacher candidates participating in the GWU/Pew Project who have successfully completed the certification process has been very favorable (approximately 70% of the candidates have achieved NBPTS certification). More than 4,000 teachers in the United States are currently nationally certified. Today, almost quadruple that number are seeking certification. As the number of teachers seeking national certification increases, so does the realization that there is a need to share information about what has or has not worked in assisting candidates to become certified.

From the beginning, as we supported candidates seeking NBPTS certification, we recognized that the process was different from the traditional teacher preparation and professional development programs designed to prepare and enhance the professional growth of teachers. We quickly realized that there were few, if any, programs to which experienced teachers could turn for support as they worked their way through the portfolio and assessment processes. We realized that as teacher educators, we, too, were learners. Thus, part of our goal has been to support teachers and another part has been to learn from this support process.

Five years of experience has brought us to the point where we believe sharing our model of supporting teachers seeking national certification is timely, appropriate, and, we hope, beneficial to others. We realize that other models are emerging. Part of our effort encourages colleges and universities, school districts, teachers' unions, and others involved in supporting the national certification process to share their experiences.

This book was written by people who have had firsthand experiences working within, and as part of, the NBPTS certification process. Its purpose is to serve as a guide for colleges and universities, school districts, organizations, or individual teachers who desire to expand and enhance the support of high levels of competence in the teaching profession, including the NBPTS certification of teachers. Part of its purpose is also one of equity: to ensure that all teachers, regardless of the level at which they teach, their content field, or whether they teach in a rural, urban, or suburban district, will be supported in their efforts to become NBPTS certified. Its purpose is to ensure that ultimately all children will have access to accomplished teachers and teaching.

The primary authors of this book are faculty members in the GWU Graduate School of Education and Human Development who worked collaboratively with professional development personnel from Virginia's Fairfax County Public Schools and other districts to design this Collaborative Model of Support. The model has successfully enabled GWU to inform, recruit, and support a growing number of teachers seeking certification. The authors, in their roles as faculty in the Department of Teacher Preparation and Special Education, are working to ensure that the teacher preparation programs have as their core the five NBPTS propositions that define what accomplished teachers should know and be able to do. We believe that all teachers, especially as we prepare to recruit more than one million new teachers within the next decade, whether they plan to become nationally certified or not, should demonstrate that they can address the core propositions and meet the standards in the various certification fields.

The authors were joined in the writing of this book by National Board Certified Teachers (NBCTs) who are now collaborating to support new teacher candidates. NBCTs are in a unique position to support the efforts of their colleagues seeking certification. These teachers have firsthand experience analyzing, understanding, and successfully completing the NBPTS certification process. They have demonstrated their ability to meet rigorous standards within their disciplines and to model exemplary teaching.

We encourage you to become part of the renaissance to reform schools and schools of education. We invite you to use part or all of this book as a guide to build systems of support that will better ensure that teachers and teacher educators are prepared to educate all Americans to their fullest potential.

MARY HATWOOD FUTRELL
Dean, Graduate School of Education
and Human Development
George Washington University
Washington, DC

Preface

The school reform movement has ignored the obvious: What teachers know and can do makes the critical difference in what children learn. Student learning in this country will improve only when we focus our efforts on improving teaching.

—NATIONAL COMMISSION ON TEACHING
AND AMERICA'S FUTURE (1996, p. 7)

In the 1980s educators, parents, business executives, and legislators awakened to the consequences of an education system that was failing to keep pace with a changing American and global society (NBPTS, 1999). The demands of an increasingly complex culture and growing diversity in the nation's student population were requiring schools to meet extraordinary new challenges.

In 1987 the Carnegie Forum on Education and the Economy's Task Force on Teaching as a Profession released *A Nation Prepared: Teachers for the 21st Century*, which focused on the role of teachers in increasing the effectiveness of schools. Based upon the recommendations of that report, representatives of a broad-based education community that included teachers, education association leaders, administrators, higher education faculty, business leaders, and parents, jointly established the National Board for Professional Teaching Standards (NBPTS). It set standards for what accomplished teachers should know and be able to do. These standards have guided the development of an assessment process designed to identify highly accomplished teachers.

The exemplary practices of National Board Certified Teachers (NBCTs), evidenced through conference presentations, journal articles, and recognition by state and national leaders, have increased interest and commitment from states and localities across the country to encourage their own teachers to become certified. But like many educational changes, the mere establishment of criteria does not ensure individuals are well prepared to meet them. Educators are increasingly becoming aware that they have a significant role to play in assisting NBPTS candidates. At the same time they recognize that there are few related resources for those who seek to support those teachers in their efforts. This book is written for facilitators—university and school professionals who are seeking guidance as they approach work with candidates during the certification process. It presents a replicable model of support and offers examples from selected certification fields that allow for generalization to other fields.

Over the past several years our experience in recruiting and supporting NBPTS candidates, as well as the findings of related research, indicate that developing a collaborative support process between university faculty, professional development personnel, and teachers is a highly effective means of assisting a teacher candidate in the successful completion of the NBPTS process.

This book goes beyond NBPTS-published materials to specifically respond to questions we have received about how to effectively support teachers. We believe that there are several essential aspects to that support:

1. **The facilitator must be well versed in the history of the NBPTS and its current practice.** Since the NBPTS process represents a shift in the efforts to examine teaching as a profession, facilitators can put the entire process in the context of the broader issues of school reform. The NBPTS is a new effort (the first certification areas were introduced in 1994) and the process is modified yearly as the NBPTS gains more experience. By operating from an understanding of the structure of the NBPTS, facilitators can readily make adjustments when changes are made. Chapter 1 provides brief background information on the NBPTS, the NBPTS certification process, and the sources available to facilitators to remain current concerning the ongoing activities of the NBPTS.

2. **Facilitators should be aware that survey research with NBPTS candidates was significant for the development of the support model and for ongoing work with the NBPTS.** We have outlined research related to the model of support presented in this book. The research provides the framework for a tested approach to supporting NBPTS candidates. This research has informed work at the university level with pre-service teachers and with practicing teachers participating in professional development training. Work with NBPTS candidates and NBCTs provides the foundation for future research about practice.

3. **Models that support NBPTS teacher candidates should be collaborative and linked to practice, research, and reflection.** Developing a model that is facilitated by content experts from universities, professional development personnel, and/or accomplished NBCTs enhances the collaborative aspect of the NBPTS assessment process. Chapter 2 presents the model in detail and provides the framework for the remainder of the book.

4. **Understanding the NBPTS assessment process in some specific certification fields enhances the effectiveness of the facilitator.** Chapters 3 through 7 focus on various aspects of the certification process. While the NBPTS eventually plans to have certificates available in 30 fields, they currently offer 16. Our work with candidates in five of the fields and with the NBPTS on the development of other fields provides insights into the similarities across fields. Therefore, we feel comfortable in providing four fields of certification as "case studies" to demonstrate the similarities and the differences. The examples may be generalized in many cases to other fields. Responses unique to one certification field are so noted.

All certification areas have six entries in the portfolio. Two of those areas always involve student work, two always involve videotaping, and two will consistently request documentation of teacher work with parents, the community, and the profession. The case study examples are from Early Childhood/Generalist (ages 3–8, general content); Early Adolescence/Generalist (teachers of ages 11–15 in an integrated setting); Early Adolescence/English Language Arts (teachers of ages 11–15, specific content); and Adolescence/Young Adulthood/Mathematics (high school, ages 14–18+, specific content).

5. **The National Board process offers an example of the continuum of teacher development.** The NBPTS assessment process can provide benchmarks for excellent practice leading to

its potential use in university pre-service education, to staff professional development at the school level, and to standards of measurement for master teachers.

6. **Facilitators need to be aware of the role NBCTs can play in local schools and the impact of the NBPTS movement on the national discussion about school reform.** Just as the historical context for the development of the NBPTS is important, at the other end of the process candidates must know how they and their collaborators may conduct research and participate as leaders in ways that continue the work of advancing the teaching profession. This NBPTS movement exists within the broader environment of educational reform. We conclude our book with some of the ways that facilitators and NBCTs may work within that context.

STRUCTURE OF THE BOOK

Chapter 1 provides the facilitator with a general overview of the NBPTS and responses to the most commonly asked questions about NBPTS certification. Additionally, it reviews the research findings that underlie the remainder of the book.

Chapter 2 presents the Collaborative Model of Support and discusses its three phases of support: Pre-Candidacy (Part I), Candidacy (Part II), and Post-Candidacy (Part III). Chapter 3 focuses on the Pre-Candidacy phase of the model, primarily on the introductory seminar in several variations. The seminar provides a format to explain the NBPTS assessment process to interested teachers and to encourage them to become candidates. Chapter 3 includes a detailed syllabus, suggested activities, related resources, and overhead masters.

Part II (Chapters 4, 5, 6, and 7) focuses on the Candidacy phase of the model. The contributors to these chapters are NBCTs, certified in the fields they discuss. The authors present information about each required portfolio entry, the standards addressed in each entry, helpful hints for completing the entries, sample activities, and resources that facilitators may use in developing support for candidates. The introduction to Part II provides general hints for facilitators, a section on videotaping hints, and information about preparation for the assessment center. This section applies to all facilitators, no matter the certification field of the candidates they are supporting.

Part III (Chapters 8 and 9) addresses the Post-Candidacy phase of the model. Chapter 8 discusses encouraging and extending teacher leadership. As the teachers become collaborators in supporting new candidates, the cyclical nature of the model is reinforced. Teacher candidates are at the center of this chapter and provide responses to such questions as: Why is this process important?, What is the impact on teachers and teacher leadership?, and What is the impact on students and learning? Chapter 9 places the NBPTS certification process in the larger context of school reform, including the impact of NBPTS certification on teachers as professionals and the impact of the NBPTS standards on teacher preparation.

This is a book about a collaborative process, one written through collaboration. We welcome feedback on its use with candidates. Its goal is to reduce the amount of "reinvention" required to effectively assist excellent teachers as they demonstrate their practice and seek NBPTS certification.

KATHLEEN ANDERSON STEEVES
BARBARA COLE BROWNE

REFERENCES

Carnegie Forum on Education and the Economy, Task Force on Teaching as a Profession. (1986). *A nation prepared: Teachers for the 21st century.* New York: Author.

National Board for Professional Teaching Standards (NBPTS). (1999). *What every teacher should know: The national board certification process 1999–2000.* Southfield, MI: Author.

National Commission on Teaching and America's Future. (1996). *What matters most: Teaching for America's future.* New York: Author.

Acknowledgments

We would like to thank the following people and organizations:

Mary Futrell, whose commitment to the mission of the National Board for Professional Teaching Standards (NBPTS) provided the framework for the collaboration that undergirds this book, and Maxine Freund, whose ongoing support and encouragement continues the George Washington University NBPTS efforts.

Our colleagues on the George Washington University/Norfolk State Partnership Advisory Board, who guided and kept alive the collaborative vision.

Contributing authors and NBPTS candidate teachers, whose collective wisdom, insights, and expertise provided a dimension to this work that would not otherwise have been possible.

Cynthia Webb-Manly and Jane Scully for their patience and expertise in editing the manuscript.

The Pew Charitable Trusts, without whose grant assistance our work with candidates would not have been possible.

KATHLEEN ANDERSON STEEVES
BARBARA COLE BROWNE

Contents

PART III. POST-CANDIDACY

PREPARING TEACHERS FOR NATIONAL BOARD CERTIFICATION

Introduction

Overview of NBPTS
and Candidate Support Research

KATHLEEN ANDERSON STEEVES
BARBARA COLE BROWNE

Chapter 1 provides facilitators with:

- Key information to describe the history, underlying goals, and process of the National Board for Professional Teaching Standards.
- A review of research findings on teacher support and its links to the Collaborative Model of Support used in this book.
- Resources for further information about the NBPTS.

QUESTIONS ABOUT NBPTS

Facilitators need to have an understanding of the National Board for Professional Teaching Standards (NBPTS), its mission, core propositions, assessment system, and importance to teachers and the teaching profession. When we present our introduction to the NBPTS to teachers, school administrators, and teacher educators, we are always asked similar questions.

What Is the National Board for Professional Teaching Standards and What Are Its Goals?

The NBPTS at a Glance

- The NBPTS is a nonprofit, *independent organization of teachers* and other education stakeholders working to advance the effectiveness of the teaching profession and improve student learning.

- The NBPTS encourages *collaboration* among all segments of the education community to mobilize support for teachers interested in meeting high and rigorous standards.
- Teachers *volunteer* to become candidates for NBPTS certification, a process that requires them to document their mastery of their content area and a variety of teaching skills and to demonstrate their professional teaching excellence.
- The NBPTS can be easily reached either by calling 1-800-22-TEACH or by accessing their website: www.nbpts.org

The NBPTS's Mission

The NBPTS's mission is:

> to establish high and rigorous standards for what accomplished teachers should know and be able to do, to develop and operate a national voluntary system to assess and certify teachers who meet these standards, and to advance related education reforms for the purpose of improving student learning in American schools. (NBPTS, 1999a)

The NBPTS's Core Propositions

Five core propositions guide the development of the standards for all areas of certification:

- Teachers are committed to students and their learning.
- Teachers know the subjects they teach and how to teach those subjects to their students.
- Teachers are responsible for managing and monitoring student learning.
- Teachers think systematically about their practice and learn from experience.
- Teachers are members of learning communities. (NBPTS, 1999b)

NBPTS Certificates Available as of 1999–2000

Teachers, teacher educators, and subject experts worked together to develop the advanced standards for each certification field. The following certificates are available as of 1999–2000.

Early Childhood (student ages 3–8)
- Generalist

Middle Childhood (student ages 7–12)
- Generalist

Early and Middle Childhood (student ages 3–12)
- English as a New Language

Early Childhood through Young Adulthood (student ages 3–18+)
- Exceptional Needs/Generalist

Early Adolescence (student ages 11–15)
- Generalist
- English Language Arts
- Mathematics
- Science
- Social Studies–History

Adolescence and Young Adulthood (student ages 14–18+)
- English Language Arts
- Mathematics
- Science
- Social Studies–History

Early Adolescence through Young Adulthood (student ages 11–18+)
- Art
- English as a New Language
- Vocational Education

The NBPTS plans to increase the number of certification fields to over 30 over the next decade. Additional fields will include:

Middle Childhood (student ages 7–12)
- English Language Arts
- Mathematics
- Science
- Social Studies–History

Early and Middle Childhood (student ages 3–12)
- Art
- Foreign Language
- Guidance Counseling
- Library/Media
- Music
- Physical Education

Early Adolescence through Young Adulthood (student ages 11–18+)
- Foreign Language
- Guidance Counseling
- Health
- Library/Media
- Music
- Physical Education

What Is the Assessment Process?

Teachers and those who support them are very much interested in what teachers are asked to do to "prove" their competence. The NBPTS assessment process is designed to reinforce authentic teaching practice that is grounded in a strong knowledge base. The process highlights teacher collaboration, creativity, reflective practice, critical thinking, and more.

Candidates seeking NBPTS certification participate in a two-part assessment process consisting of creation of a portfolio and assessment center activities. All components of the assessment are performance-based and provide candidates with the opportunity to demonstrate their knowledge, skills, and ability to promote student learning.

The first part of the assessment involves the candidate's creation of a school site–based portfolio that documents the candidate's teaching strategies and student work through written commentaries, videotapes, teaching artifacts, examples of student work, and analysis of classroom activities. The portfolio consists of six entries, four of which relate to the classroom, and two, called "Documented Accomplishments," that demonstrate teacher relationships to student parents, the community at large, and the profession.

The second part of the assessment process requires the candidate to participate in assessment center exercises completed at a locality designated by the NBPTS. (Currently, Sylvan Learning Centers are being used as the location for this phase of the assessment process.) The exercises are designed to complement the work demonstrated in the portfolio and to involve the teacher candidate in challenging teaching issues across the designated field of certification. Assessment center activities are scheduled by the teacher candidate following her or his submission of the school site–based portfolio; these activities are completed in one day.

A candidate's entire assessment process, from receiving the portfolio information, to gathering the required documentation, to completing the activities at the assessment center site takes the better part of a school year. Teachers who have completed the process report spending time equivalent to that involved in taking a graduate-level course.

Similarities across All Certification Fields

1. All portfolios require six entries:

   - Four entries are classroom-based
   - Two of these entries involve student work
   - Two of these entries involve videotapes of practice

2. All portfolios have two entries demonstrating candidate relationships to parents, community, and profession.
3. All six entries require written commentary that offers clear, concise, and convincing evidence.
4. Assessment center activities are completed after submission of the portfolio.
5. All activities are grounded in the five core propositions, although specific standards are written for each certification field.
6. Standards are the lens through which the portfolio and assessment center responses are measured.

Unique Demands for Each Certificate Field

Each certificate field has its own requirements as well, depending upon the student age range for the certificate and whether it is a generalist or content-focused certificate. While there is not time or space in this book to illustrate all of the differences, some examples can be found in the chapters that address specific certificates.

For example, those who are seeking Early Childhood/Generalist certification (Chapter 4) will be expected not only to speak to the needs of young children, but also to be able to demonstrate a knowledge of how to create a learning environment that is interdisciplinary; perhaps including social studies concepts in a reading lesson. By contrast, the Adolescence/Young Adulthood/Mathematics certification candidates (Chapter 7) are expected to demonstrate in-depth knowledge of five domains of mathematics and be able to construct and evaluate simple and complex mathematics lessons for older students with varying mathematics knowledge.

What Are the Requirements for Candidacy?

To be eligible to apply for NBPTS candidacy, a teacher must hold a baccalaureate degree, must have a minimum of three years' teaching experience, and must have held a valid state teaching license for those three years. Where a license is not required, the teacher must have taught in schools recognized and approved to operate by the state—for example, private K–12 schools that meet the state criteria for a teaching license. The potential candidate must be teaching in or have continual contact with two to three classes of students in the certification field in which he or she intends to seek certification.

Why Is NBPTS Certification Important to Teachers and the Teaching Profession?

Successful candidates report that the process provided them with an opportunity to grow professionally; to demonstrate their skills, knowledge, and talents; and to work collaboratively with school and university peers. In the words of teachers who have participated in the Collaborative Model of Support, the experience provided:

- "Professional growth where it really happens—in my classroom with my students."
- "The opportunity for serious reflection and self-examination, as I gauge my skills and knowledge against objective, peer-developed, national standards in specific teaching areas."
- "The prospect of increased mobility, rewards, and career opportunities."
- "Professional recognition for demonstrating highly accomplished teaching practice."

RESEARCH ON NBPTS SUPPORT MODEL

The research findings presented here are the result of interviews with teachers whom the authors have supported through collaboration over the past four years as candidates for NBPTS certification (Futrell & Rotberg, 1998). The findings have been used to measure the success of our model of support. Additionally, they have been used to guide our efforts to expand the cyclical nature of the NBPTS process in our ongoing work in promoting change in teacher education. The Collaborative Model of Support and the structure presented in this book are guided by this research.

Of greatest importance for facilitators are the 10 major factors our research has identified as crucial for a teacher to be successful in his or her NBPTS candidacy. While some factors refer to the teacher candidates and some to facilitators, all our findings provide important information that needs to be considered while supporting teachers as they seek NBPTS certification.

1. **Facilitators need to be familiar with the NBPTS standards and its assessment process.** Facilitators need to provide candidates with guidance about how best to approach the assessment process. In order to be most effective, the facilitator's knowledge about the NBPTS process must be complete and up-to-date. Facilitators should be able to keep candidates on track, provide critical feedback, answer questions about the standards and the process, help in obtaining technical equipment or content specific resources, and be current in teaching methodology, research, and theory.

2. **Facilitators need to help candidates understand NBPTS expectations regarding all portfolio entries and provide candidates with opportunities to practice.** Candidates will need to be familiar with the NBPTS standards for their specific certification field and to understand what is required by each standard as it applies to the portfolio entries. They will need encouragement to think critically about what they do in their classroom that demonstrates how they meet the standards. When viewed as a whole, the portfolio process can be daunting. By breaking the process down into individual entries, and linking it with the required standards, the facilitator can assist the candidates by giving them a clearer picture of what is required for each entry and by creating opportunities to practice their understanding. (Chapters 3 through 7 are particularly relevant to this process.)

3. **Candidates must evaluate their time commitments.** The facilitator should assist candidates in breaking complex portfolio requirements into discrete, manageable tasks. We have found that candidates benefit from the development of a timeline (see Figure 2.2 for a sample timeline). We have also found those candidates who cleared their school-year calendar of additional duties, started early, and paced themselves were more effective.

4. **Support from peers and administrators is very important for candidates.** Candidates should be encouraged to seek support from building or system administrators (i.e., content specialists, principals, superintendents) and other teachers. Candidates need others to talk with, to provide them with feedback, and to answer their questions.

5. **Facilitators should organize support sessions and hold them throughout the entire certification process.** Working with another candidate as a partner or in a small group provides opportunities for valuable collaboration with peers. The support sessions are also helpful for candidates as places to ask or answer questions, to give and receive feedback, to ask for or to provide technical assistance, and to stay on track. Support sessions should be held weekly or biweekly, should be candidate-driven, and should be informal in tone. Teachers tend to do better when they work in small groups on the same item. Groups that are made up of teachers in the same certification field are the most helpful in determining if candidates are "on track" and are "making connections to the standards" in their writing.

6. **Facilitators should encourage candidates to develop and refine their reflective and analytical skills.** A significant part of the response to the portfolio entries involves reflection and analysis of lessons, student work, and the like. Candidates must have the opportunity to practice reflecting on their own lessons and analyzing their own classroom practice, as well as the lessons and practice of others. "Peer observation" and substantive small-group discussions with other candidates facilitate this practice.

7. **Facilitators must provide candidates with opportunities to write about teaching.** Our work with candidates revealed that many candidates who did not achieve certification had difficulty translating the theory and practice of their teaching into their written commentaries. Thus it is essential for facilitators to organize writing seminars or the like to assist candidates in improving their critical writing.

8. **Facilitators must assist candidates in evaluating and enhancing their knowledge base in their certification fields.** Candidates must be up-to-date concerning research on teaching in their chosen certification field. Candidates need to be knowledgeable about current research on the student age group and the content area for their certification field. Facilitators can assist candidates in developing resources specific to the research and theory in their field by encouraging them to read professional journals, to survey curriculum materials, and to familiarize themselves with current jargon, educational trends, and different teaching strategies.

9. **Facilitators should provide opportunities for candidates to practice videotaping their classrooms and then to analyze their videotapes.** All portfolios require two videotaped entries.

Thus, candidates *must* become comfortable working with video equipment. Beginning early in the certification process, facilitators should help candidates to learn about the videotaping process, to practice videotaping, and to analyze the tapes they make.

10. **Facilitators must share how each portfolio entry is evaluated with candidates.** The NBPTS has considerable information on how they score all aspects of the assessment. These evaluation guidelines should be examined by facilitators and shared with candidates, to guide their responses and further their study and work with facilitators and peers.

These 10 factors identified by candidates themselves are crucial for facilitators to keep in mind as they support candidates seeking NBPTS certification. We have integrated those factors into the Collaborative Model of Support we use as a framework for this book.

REFERENCES

Futrell, M. H., & Rotberg, I. (1998). *Unpublished research report.* Philadelphia, PA: Pew Charitable Trusts.

National Board for Professional Teaching Standards. (1999a, April). *Backgrounder.* Detroit: Author.

National Board for Professional Teaching Standards. (1999b). *What every teacher should know: The National Board Certification Process 1999–2000.* Southfield, MI: Author.

PART ONE

Pre-Candidacy

The Collaborative Model of Teacher Support

BARBARA COLE BROWNE

KATHLEEN ANDERSON STEEVES

> Not only do teachers need time and opportunity to reflect on their
> work, they need that time and opportunity to do so in the company
> of others with whom they can construct meaning.
> —LAMBERT, COLLEY, DIETZ, KENT, AND RECHERT (1996, p. 161)

Chapter 2 provides facilitators with:

- An understanding of the components of the Collaborative Model of Support.
- The ability to replicate all or parts of the model.
- Insights into how to provide support to NBPTS candidates.

The Collaborative Model of Support presented in this chapter provides a tested replicable model that enables facilitators to develop programs for supporting NBPTS candidates in their community. The model may be used in its entirety or its components can be adapted to the special needs of the facilitator.

We will begin by offering a detailed description of the Collaborative Model of Teacher Support: this model provides the organizational framework for the remainder of the book. The model is divided into three phases: Pre-Candidacy, Candidacy, and Post-Candidacy. The specific contents of each phase are laid out in Figure 2.1. Keep in mind that the model makes constant use of collaboration in all its components and that the process is cyclical. Individuals may begin as NBPTS candidates, become National Board Certified Teachers (NBCTs), then serve as recruiters,

---

Build a Community Network of Key Collaborators—University Faculty, School Personnel, NBCTs

Phase 1: Pre Candidacy
- Disseminate Information and Recruit Candidates
- Pre-Candidacy Preparation (see Chapters 1, 2, and 3)

Phase 2: Candidacy
- Portfolio Support Seminars
- Assessment Center Support (see Chapters 4, 5, 6, and 7)

Phase 3: Post-Candidacy
- Candidate Recognition
- Reflective Group Activities
- Leadership Opportunities
- Link to Research (see Chapters 8 and 9)

FIGURE 2.1. Collaborative model of teacher support.

and finally become facilitators; facilitators may train pre-service teachers in NBPTS core propositions and standards, assist experienced teachers in becoming NBPTS, and work with NBCTs in school/university partnerships.

DEVELOPING A COMMUNITY NETWORK

Involving a broad-based network of leaders within the education community who can participate in preparing and supporting NBPTS candidates increases the effectiveness of the model.

The community network, which could include university faculty, school personnel, teachers, and candidates, provides a vehicle to disseminate information and coordinate efforts related to the NBPTS assessment process. To avoid duplication of efforts, facilitators should consider enlisting the help of the following personnel when designing support systems for NBPTS candidates:

University Faculty

Faculty who have expertise in the current NBPTS certification fields can enhance candidates' content knowledge, support them, and consult with them. Faculty can also be helpful in encouraging supervising teachers in the schools where university students are placed for internships to seek NBPTS certification.

Additionally, university faculty can promote the NBPTS and recruit teachers by encouraging their own graduates to seek certification at the point in their careers when they meet NBPTS requirements. Partnerships between universities and area schools can coordinate the continuum of teacher preparation and ongoing professional development programs by using the NBPTS standards as a framework. NBCTs from partner schools can serve as mentors for pre-service teachers. Today, more and more universities across the country are aligning pre-service programs with NBPTS core propositions and certificate standards. This realignment should result in a new generation of teachers and NBPTS candidates who will be prepared for the NBPTS assessment process. Universities in the same geographic area may establish their own network to exchange ideas and support each other's NBPTS efforts.

P–12 School Personnel

School board members, superintendents, principals, staff development personnel, and other school personnel can be enlisted to provide direct support for those teachers who are seeking NBPTS certification. Each of these groups has a unique position from which to develop opportunities and incentives for teachers. Facilitators should be aware of the incentives and support candidates receive from their schools. Examples of school system support include paying the application fee for any teacher seeking NBPTS certification, recognizing NBCTs as outstanding teachers, and paying for substitute teachers to allow NBPTS candidates time to develop their portfolios.

Community

State and local businesses, legislators, parent–teacher associations, and others can both offer their direct support to NBPTS candidates and advocate for incentives related to NBPTS efforts. For example, a local city council recently set aside $20,000 to pay fees ($2,000 per teacher) for teachers going through the NBPTS assessment process. Some states pay part or all of a candidate's fee and provide a bonus and other monetary rewards for those who achieve certification. The NBPTS maintains an up-to-date list of incentives available to candidates.

School and Education Organizations

Teacher-related networks such as teacher organizations (e.g., the National Education Association, the American Federation of Teachers, and local groups), and content organizations, such as the International Reading Association, the National Council of Teachers of Mathematics, the National Association for the Education of Young Children, or the Council for Exceptional Children/Division of Early Childhood are resources for recruitment, content knowledge, and related resource support for each certification field. Additionally, these organizations provide networks for national, state, and local advocacy efforts to improve incentives for those seeking NBPTS certification. For example, using many of the components of this model, the Virginia Education Association has collaborated with the Virginia Department of Education, state school districts, in-state universities, and NBCTs to develop a statewide system for supporting NBPTS teacher candidates.

National Board Certified Teachers

Facilitators should work closely with NBCTs who have experienced the assessment process because they are key players in developing support models. As teachers achieve NBPTS certification, they become leaders both in recruiting others and providing support for new candidates. For example, many NBCTs serve as facilitators in the Pre-Candidacy introductory seminar that initiates the candidacy process.

Part or all of this diverse network can be used to construct the community that recruits, prepares, and supports successful NBPTS candidates.

Figure 2.2 offers a timeline delineating the three phases of support and when they may be implemented.

Phase	Activities timeline			
Pre-Candidacy	When Jan.–April	What Recruitment and information meetings Chapter 2	Why To inform teachers; to get superintendents, principals, and community network involved	Who Facilitators: university faculty, staff development personnel, National Board Certified Teachers
	May–Sept.	Information meetings (mini-seminar, three- to six-hour workshop) Chapter 2	To inform teachers and conduct mini-seminar, provide overview of NBPTS assessment process	Facilitators
	Sept.–Oct.	Introductory Seminar (five-week workshop) Chapter 3	To provide teachers with an in-depth understanding of the assessment process	Facilitators
Candidacy	Oct.–June	Support Sessions Chapters 2, 4–7	To provide candidates support and feedback during NBPTS assessment process	Facilitators
Post-Candidacy	June–Oct.	Candidacy; recognition reflective group Chapters 2, 8	To highlight benefits and challenges of assessment; to discuss future support; to recognize candidate teacher accomplishments	Facilitators

FIGURE 2.2. Collaborative model of teacher support.

THE PRE-CANDIDACY PHASE

The Pre-Candidacy phase provides facilitators with the opportunity to disseminate information about the NBPTS, to recruit candidates, and to conduct an introductory seminar. The purpose of pre-candidacy is to assist candidates in determining if they are ready (in terms of skills, knowledge, and time) for the NBPTS assessment process. This phase occurs before teachers have made a final commitment to the NBPTS assessment process.

Dissemination of Information and Recruitment

Providing information about the NBPTS assessment process and recruiting candidates is a prime example of the necessity of collaboration. Working together, people from universities, schools, and other institutions can expand the reach of a single group. If financial resources to support NBPTS candidates are limited, innovative practices to compensate facilitators for their time and expertise may need to be considered. For example, faculty may be allowed to use the time spent as facilitators as a portion of their service obligation. Foundations and businesses may be asked to provide financial resources. Schools may incorporate their recruitment into already scheduled systemwide meetings and ask university faculty to present a session on the benefits of NBPTS candidacy.

The facilitator needs to take primary responsibility for coordinating and hosting initial information sessions for all who are interested, be they staff development personnel, superintendents, or teacher association officers. The most effective recruitment efforts occur when school systems and a university combine their efforts to reach out to potential candidates. As the number of NBCTs increases, the collaboration extends beyond recruitment, to presentations at conferences and information sessions and outreach to their peers.

Facilitators can expand recruitment efforts in the following manner:

- Education associations and professional organizations may disseminate information about NBPTS certification opportunities via newsletters, journal articles, and local, regional, and state meetings. These organizations have the potential to reach large numbers of teachers and administrators at all levels.
- University collaborators can send information to their graduates and to their internship supervisors/cooperating teachers to reach potential candidates.
- A group of universities and colleges can establish a network to coordinate information and strategies for recruitment and support of teachers.
- University faculty can present information about the NBPTS in their education classes.

Pre-Candidacy Preparation

Introductory Seminar

Once enough teachers indicate an initial interest in pursuing NBPTS certification, facilitators can offer the introductory seminar. This seminar's main purpose is to guide the potential candidate toward a clear understanding of the standards and core propositions of the NBPTS, and to explain what the assessment process entails. This helps prospective candidates evaluate how their own teaching reflects these propositions and standards and determine their readiness to participate.

In particular, the seminar provides teachers with a preview of the skills and knowledge they will need for pursuing NBPTS certification by developing their school-based portfolios (Part 1) and by participating in the assessment center (Part 2). When they complete the seminar, teachers should know whether they are prepared to begin the NBPTS assessment process or whether they are not ready to go ahead at this time.

A detailed syllabus for a 15-hour introductory seminar developed by NBCTs and university faculty is presented in Chapter 3. We highly recommend the content included in the seminar syllabus, but we also recognize that facilitators may need to revise this content and establish their own timeline for completing the activities. At a minimum, the seminar should provide enough information and practice to enable teachers to decide if they are prepared to pursue NBPTS certification.

Mini-Workshop

A shorter version (mini-workshop) of the full seminar can provide basic information about the NBPTS certification process. We support either a three- or a six-hour format, using portions of the full introductory seminar content (see Appendix 3.2, Chapter 3).

University and Professional Development Programs

Many universities have developed individual courses and even whole programs that provide an introduction to the NBPTS, and/or relate the pedagogy and content of their programs to the core propositions of the NBPTS. Many of these efforts are collaborative and include university faculty, professional development programs in schools, and/or teacher associations. All of these efforts are designed to increase the skills and knowledge of teachers so that they will be better prepared if and when they decide to engage in the NBPTS assessment process. Further discussion of the efforts emerging across the continuum of teacher preparation can be found in Chapter 9.

THE CANDIDACY PHASE

Teachers who have completed the introductory seminar, who feel confident about their skills and knowledge, and who choose to commit to the NBPTS certification process, may apply directly to the NBPTS to become a candidate for certification. After receiving payment of its fee (currently $2,000 but scheduled to increase in 2000/2001), the NBPTS sends the candidate materials containing the directions for developing her or his portfolio.

The portfolio for each certification field requires candidates to address six entries that involve written commentaries, videotapes, and artifacts that document their teaching. Four entries are directly related to classroom practice and two entries relate to family, community, and professional partnerships.

As soon as the candidates receive their NBPTS materials, the facilitator should initiate support services. Our research indicates that this support enhances the professional development of candidates and increases successful completion of the assessment. Repeated comments from candidates stressed the value of such external support to their candidacy. For example:

> "It was very clear that I was one person and needed additional perspectives in order to get through the process, to fully flesh out the standards and see how they were demonstrated in the classroom."—NBCT, Early Adolescence/Generalist

As we mentioned earlier, the NBPTS certification process itself has two components: creation of a portfolio based on work done at the school site and successful completion of a series of activities at an assessment center. Ideally, support that is specific to each certification field begins during the development of the portfolio and continues as the candidate prepares for the assessment center. In Chapters 4, 5, 6, and 7 of this book NBCTs provide hints for facilitators and examples of activities in four certification fields. We selected these fields because they provide generalizibility for facilitators working across the age ranges and with different content areas.

Portfolio Development: Support Group Sessions

The purpose of support sessions during the development of the portfolio is to provide teacher candidates with an opportunity to meet together, to collaborate, and to expand their experiences. Such sessions should begin soon after the candidate receives the portfolio materials, when he or she is starting the task of describing and documenting actual teaching practices.

Role of the Facilitator

The facilitator's role at this stage is to organize and lead the support groups. The facilitators in the initial Collaborative Model of Support were two university faculty members who worked in conjunction with school professional development personnel. As teachers became NBPTS certified, they took on the role of primary facilitators, although they relied on continued assistance from university and school personnel. In the Collaborative Model of Support, the format of the support sessions—who participates, what topics are discussed, and the frequency of meetings—is chosen by the candidates. Early in the process, the candidates and the facilitators preview the portfolio materials for their varying certification fields, develop timelines, and discuss procedural issues that need clarification.

Seminar Logistics

When given the choice, teachers consistently choose to meet regularly during the portfolio development phase. Initially, they meet one or two times per month, then, as the portfolio due date nears, with increasing frequency. Our candidates met in small groups (four to six teachers) in specific certification areas (e.g., Early Childhood/Generalist or Adolescence Young Adulthood/ Mathematics). Occasionally they decided to meet in a large group (cross-certification fields) to address issues that were similar across all certificates, such as the logistics of videotaping classroom activities or how best to do reflective writing.

Content of Support Sessions

The content of the support sessions was determined by the candidates themselves. The nature of the content varied, depending on the certification field and where the candidates were in the development of their portfolios. Whereas some sessions might focus on specific academic disciplines (e.g., English language arts, mathematics), others might focus on assessment techniques or the theory of inquiry teaching. Our experience reveals that the Documented Accomplishments entries are a good place to begin the support sessions. These entries are included in the portfolios for all certificates.

We have used the following activities in all our support groups to address the needs of the candidates and to encourage collaboration among facilitators and candidates. Figure 2.3 synthesizes the main components. A sample syllabus can be found in Appendix 2.1.

SUBSTANTIVE DISCUSSIONS

Discussions regarding portfolio entry content should be an important part of each support session. The NBPTS does not demand any one instructional approach or advocate any one teaching philosophy. Therefore, it is essential that each teacher candidate be able to provide clear, concise, and convincing evidence to document his or her own teaching practice in relation to the standards.

SHARING WRITTEN WORK

"In many cases, a major reason candidates are unsuccessful is that they observe, but don't analyze [in their writing]."—NBCT, Early Adolescence/Generalist

Each candidate must develop written commentaries designed to analyze his or her own teaching practice. Many candidates find that critically analyzing their own work and putting the results of this analysis into a written commentary is a challenge. The candidate may choose to share the drafts of successive written commentaries with facilitators. Candidates reveal that feedback from facilitators helps them expand their thinking and thus strengthen their written analyses. Note: the facilitator *should* only give suggestions, and *never* change or rewrite the candidate's work.

Activity	Purpose	Type of activity
Substantive discussions regarding development of portfolio entries	• Update group on progress • Discuss positive accomplishments in portfolio progress • Address challenges • Hold discussions related to content, specific entry • Share artifacts • Practice integrating standards into teaching and writing • Provide feedback on video clips and related written analysis	• Large group—may be general across certification fields • Small group—same certification field
Sharing written work	• Provide candidates with feedback on written work to expand their thinking • Link writing to standards (may note in margin the standards that are addressed) • Make suggestions regarding clarity and organization of work • Suggest resources that may expand knowledge and support teaching • Encourage candidates to "sing own praises."	• Partner pairs • Small group—facilitator and other candidates focus on one written commentary • Facilitator-written input
Collaborating with colleagues	• Share ideas and build on others' practices • Support videotaping	• E-mail, phone contact • Colleague at school (teacher, administrator, specialist) • Regular contact (daily or more when needed)

Viewing and critiquing videos
  What does the video demonstrate?
  How does it relate to the standards?
	• Observe tapes and reflect on content
	• Provide feedback on video content and quality
	• Provide feedback on teaching practice and help interpret teaching
	• Expand candidates' thinking regarding meaning of work
	• Discuss relevance of written commentary to video
	• Identify relationship to standards and evidence of standards
	• Understand process of analyzing video
		• Small group—(content-specific) (facilitators and peers)

Sharing relevant content information and research	• Share current journal articles • Identify curriculum- or content-specific resources • Gather materials and resources to provide background information and add substance to their practices	• Small and/or large group (contents specific)
Liaison to NBPTS	• Clarify questions related to the assessment process	• Facilitator serves as liaison—large and small group

FIGURE 2.3. Sample support session activities.

COLLABORATING WITH COLLEAGUES

Candidates who have participated in our Collaborative Model report that it was helpful to have a "critical friend" in their school or from the same certification field to provide them with ongoing support and feedback.

> "The most rewarding element was the professional, collaborative relationship that developed with my partner teacher. Support sessions offered opportunities for ongoing reflective practice. Not only did I reap the benefits of professional dialogue with newly appointed team members, but I was able to receive and share information with others involved in the NBPTS process."—NBCT, Early Childhood/Generalist

VIEWING AND CRITIQUING VIDEOS

"Taping is telling." Candidates for NBPTS certification are required to create videotapes to document their actual classroom practices. Facilitators can be especially helpful in providing feedback to candidates regarding this requirement. A candidate's written analysis of his or her taped segments is a key component of the portfolio. Colleagues and facilitators can work together to help the candidates identify the teaching techniques/methodologies they use and then interpret their effectiveness with students. The candidates themselves find that sharing insights about each other's practices leads to a clearer analysis of their own teaching practices. General hints on videotaping that apply to all certificates are found in the Introduction to Part II.

SHARING RELEVANT CONTENT INFORMATION AND RESEARCH

Candidates may need to update their expertise in a content area or to review the theoretical constructs that guide and add credence to interpretation and analysis of their work. University faculty with expertise in pedagogy and content related to each certification field can be especially helpful here.

LIAISON TO NBPTS

Candidates often have questions related to the development of their portfolios. At each support session facilitators should address these questions. If they are unsure of an answer, they should contact the NBPTS for clarification. By synthesizing questions from the large group and/or small groups, and then contacting the NBPTS, the facilitator saves both the candidate and the NBPTS valuable time.

Assessment Center: Candidate Support

Once the portfolio has been completed and submitted to the NBPTS, the candidates immediately begin to focus on the next phase of the process, preparing for the assessment center. During their one-day assessment, candidates in all certificate fields respond to classroom situations that address issues regarding both pedagogy and content.

Facilitators may want to individualize their preparations based on the needs of each candidate. Facilitators can work with candidates to review and update content-area information. Support sessions during this period should focus on issues beyond the candidate's own classroom. Such discussion should lead to an expansion of candidates' thoughts across the age range (e.g., ages 3 to 8 for Early Childhood/Generalist) or across the content of the certification field (e.g., algebra, trigonometry, and geometry for Adolescence/Young Adulthood/Mathematics). Support sessions help teachers to update and expand their content knowledge and to read about and discuss pedagogical issues. Samples of resources and specific content information for this phase can be found in Chapters 4 through 7.

THE POST-CANDIDACY PHASE

This support phase is discussed in much greater detail in Chapter 8.

Candidate Recognition

Candidates work hard to complete the NBPTS assessment process. It is important to celebrate the work and accomplishments of all candidates who complete the process. Therefore, we recommend recognition of all teachers following completion of the portfolio and assessment center process, before the candidates have actually been notified about the results (usually in November). Our experience indicates that bringing the candidates together for a reception that includes peers from their schools and their principals (with the candidates' permission) is a positive way to celebrate the completion of the NBPTS process.

Reflective Group Activity

During the NBPTS assessment process, candidates work intensely in collaborative groups and thus form a strong, cohesive support network with their colleagues. Yet the reality is that some candidates who complete the process do not achieve certification the first time. Thus, facilitators should bring the group together *before* the notification of achievement to address such guiding questions as: "What did I learn from the process?" "How did I positively change my teaching?" "How will we, as a group, support our peers who do not achieve certification the first time?" This process will assist those candidates who do not initially accrue the needed points to achieve certification and will develop a mechanism for continued support from their peers should they choose to retake portions of their assessment.

The "banking" policy established by the NBPTS helps teachers who do not initially achieve certification. Thanks to this policy, candidates may "bank" their high scores and need only retake those sections of the assessment where they showed weaknesses. At this time, candidates have up to three years to acquire the needed score to achieve NBPTS certification.

Leadership Opportunities/Research

Once the candidates are notified that they have achieved certification, the new NBCTs will have many opportunities to share their knowledge and expertise. We highly recommend that facilitators enlist new NBCTS in leadership and other educational roles. NBCTs who have participated in the Collaborative Model have had the opportunity to:

- Support other teachers as they seek NBPTS certification.
- Present in university courses.
- Collaborate with university faculty and school personnel by presenting at conferences.

- Participate as advisory team members related to local NBPTS efforts.
- Participate in local, regional, and state professional development and advocacy opportunities.
- Provide leadership roles in their own schools.
- Mentor new teachers and/or supervise student teacher interns.

NBCTs are an invaluable resource for the entire education/school community. Their work reinforces the cyclical nature of the Collaborative Model of Support as they take on leadership roles in their work with other teachers and with their own school communities to improve student learning. NBCTs are also encouraged to develop action research projects to document changes in their practice once they have achieved certification. Chapter 8 contains more comprehensive discussion of the Post-Candidacy phase of the Collaborative Model of Support and its impact on teacher leadership.

FACILITATOR INSIGHTS: NBCTs AS PARTNERS

As the Collaborative Model of Support evolved and more teachers became NBPTS certified, these teachers themselves became the primary facilitators in the model. Although university and staff development personnel continued to facilitate, they now could assist the process in other ways. Feedback from teachers going through certification revealed that they greatly valued input from NBCTs who had been through certification and understood the process. This model then developed into a process that truly emphasized the collaboration that the NBPTS promotes. It has not only encouraged reflection and provided the opportunity to better assist teachers seeking NBPTS certification, it has also improved our understanding of the NBPTS process and its impact on teacher practice and student learning. As facilitators working with candidates for the duration of this project, we identified the following specific skills and knowledge as important to achieving NBPTS certification. They have been incorporated into the Collaborative Model of Support.

- A comprehension of the NBPTS mission, its five core propositions, and specific certification field standards. This can be addressed during the introductory seminar, through the development of the portfolio, and during one-on-one and group discussions among facilitators and peers. Since the propositions and standards provide the framework for the portfolio and assessment center activities, candidates must have a clear understanding of both so that they can incorporate both in their portfolio and assessment center responses.
- The ability to describe and reflect on one's own work, to answer questions such as "What is happening in my classroom?" and "Why is this happening?" It is important to differentiate between describing *what* is happening and reflecting on *why*.
- The ability to analyze one's own teaching, that is, to be able to interpret and provide the reasons and motives for teaching choices—for example, "What evidence does the written commentary provide about my instructional choices and my students' learning?" We found that candidates can observe and describe *what* happens in their practice, but they often don't analyze and think about *why* they are teaching a certain lesson in a certain way. Facilitators should keep these concepts and questions at the forefront of the support group discussions to provide a framework that promotes analytical thinking and reflective writing.
- The ability to revise one's practice through self-analysis and to systematically evaluate

one's teaching practice. The self-analysis can be promoted by responding to the questions "What will I do differently?" and "Why?"

- The ability to write critically. This includes being able to explain, reflect, interpret, and provide documentation or evidence to support one's teaching choices. This is an area in which facilitators can become coaches and encourage clear concise writing.
- The ability to assess the needs of each student and of groups of students and to modify practice accordingly.
- The ability to understand and interpret the standards and integrate them into one's work.

A comprehensive listing of resources on pedagogy, especially reflective practice, is included at the end of this chapter.

Chapter 3 focuses on the Pre-Candidacy phase of the model and provides a detailed syllabus of the introductory seminar for facilitators to use to introduce teachers to the NBPTS.

"I realize that teachers are dynamic. I'm very different from what I was 10 years ago, or what I'll be 10 years from now."—NBCT, Early Adolescence/Generalist

RESOURCES

Adler, S. A. (1993). Teacher education: Research as reflective practice. *Teacher and Teacher Education*, 9, 159–167.

Bartz, D. E., & Miller, L. K. (1991). *Twelve teaching methods to enhance student learning*. Washington, DC: National Education Association.

Brubaker, D. L., & Simon, L. H. (1993). *Teacher as decision maker*. Newbury Park, CA: Corwin Press.

Danielson, C. (1996). *Enhancing professional practice: A framework for teaching*. Alexandria, VA: Association for Supervision and Curriculum Development.

Dieker, L. A., & Monda-Amaya, L. E. (1995). Reflective teaching: A process for analyzing journals of preservice educators. *Teacher Education and Special Education*, 18(4), 240–252.

Enz, B. J., Freeman, D. J., & Wrana, J. (1995). *Student teacher and mentor conversations: A study of the nature and impact of instructional feedback*. Paper presented at the American Educational Research Association annual meeting, San Francisco.

Estabrooke, M., & Goldsberry, L. (1995). *Learning side by side*. Paper presented at the American Educational Research Association annual meeting, San Francisco.

Freeman, N. K. (1997). Mama and Daddy taught me right from wrong—Isn't that enough? *Young Children*, 52(6), 64–67.

Henderson, J. G. (1992). *Reflective teaching and becoming an inquiring educator*. New York: Macmillan.

Karge, B. D., Lasky, B., McCabe, M., & Robb, S. M. (1995). University and district collaborative support for beginning special education intern teachers. *Teacher Education and Special Education*, 18(2), 103–114.

Langer, G. M., & Colton, A. B. (1997). *Standards-based teacher portfolios for professional growth*. Paper presented at the National Staff Development Council annual conference, Nashville, TN.

McIntyre, J. D., & Byrd, D. M. (Eds). (1998). *Strategies for career-long teacher education: Teacher education yearbook 6*. Thousand Oaks, CA: Corwin Press.

Morehead, M. A., Lyman, L., & Foyle, H. (1995). *Workshops for improving supervision of student teachers*. Washington, DC: American Association of Colleges for Teacher Education.

National Commission on Teaching and America's Future. (1996). *What matters most: Teaching and America's future*. New York: Author.

Rogers, S. (1987). If I can see myself, I can change. *Educational Leadership, 45*(2), 64–67.

Shulman, J. H., & Colbert, J. A. (1989). Cases as catalysts for cases: Including reflection in teacher education. *Action in Teacher Education, 11*(1), 44–51.

Tertell, E. A., Klein, S. M., & Jewett, J. L. (Eds). (1998). *When teachers reflect: Journeys toward effective, inclusive practice*. Washington DC: National Association for the Education of Young Children.

Wise, A. E. (1996). Shattering the status quo: The National Commission Report and teacher preparation. *The Newsletter of the National Council of Accreditation of Teacher Education, 6*(1), 1–8.

Wolf, K., Whinery, B., & Hagerty, P. (1995). Teaching portfolios and portfolio conversations for teacher educators and teachers. *Action in Teacher Education, 17*(1), 30–39.

APPENDIX 2.1
Sample Syllabus
for Support Group Sessions

Purpose

The purpose of the support group sessions is to promote collaboration among NBPTS teacher candidates; to support and encourage candidates as they develop their portfolios and prepare for the assessment center activities; and to enhance their professional development as they prepare for NBPTS certification.

Time Frame

Support sessions should begin as soon as candidates have applied for certification and received their portfolio materials. The sessions can start as early as the beginning of the school year. However, most candidates indicate that it is important for them to first get to know their students in the classes. For that reason our Collaboration Model of Support suggests that the introductory seminar (discussed in Chapter 3) be held during the summer or early fall before candidacy. The support groups can get under way as candidates receive their materials and continue until submission of the portfolios and completion of the assessment center activities.

Sample Session Topics

Session 1 Introducing the portfolio; Overview of entries; Answering general questions; Developing collaborative relationships—for example, by sharing e-mail addresses, phone numbers, and areas of certificate.

Session 2 Developing timelines; Question and answers; Understanding the standards; Selecting students for case studies.

Session 3 Videotaping logistics and requirements (e.g., permission forms); Preparing to document accomplishments; Questions and answers.

Session 4 Sharing written commentaries from documented accomplishments; Critical writing; Question and answers.

Sessions 5 through 10 Sharing entries—candidates can share which entries they would like to focus on; Linking to the standards; Feedback on written commentaries and videotapes.

Session 11 and 12 Wrapping up loose ends; What's next?—planning for the assessment center support groups.

Note. In between sessions we recommend you maintain contact with candidates through e-mail, phone calls, and individual meetings. We recommend the sessions be offered every other week to allow facilitators time to read and respond to written commentaries and candidates time to develop their entries.

The Introductory Seminar

CAROL HORN
CAROL SULTZMAN
BETTY COSTELLO

Chapter 3 provides facilitators with:

- An outline for an introductory seminar to inform interested teachers about the NBPTS assessment process.
- Detailed activities and exercises for each session.
- A resources list for facilitators.
- Overhead masters with agendas and objectives for each seminar session.

Teaching has an embedded history of isolating colleagues because of the daily demands of the field. The NBPTS experience breaks down the walls of isolation for teachers. Its certification process establishes positive steps toward collaboration among colleagues that lead to the development of a true community of learners. Such collaboration benefits teachers who are new to the assessment process as well as teachers who have already achieved NBPTS certification. The ultimate goal of the NBPTS is to improve classroom teaching and enhance student achievement.

To promote the NBPTS's mission and achieve greater collaboration, the teaching profession requires a network of NBPTS candidate support. The support network enhances the experience of individuals, improves their chances of gaining certification, and strengthens professionalism among colleagues at all levels. As an essential element in the pre-candidacy phase of the Collaborative Model of Support, we designed a seminar to provide potential candidates with an understanding of the practical realities of the NBPTS process and the effect of the process on classroom practice. This seminar is designed to introduce participants to the history, purpose, current status, and future plans of the NBPTS. Additionally, interested teachers have the opportunity throughout the seminar to engage in activities that will help them to work with others to increase their knowledge of the requirements for NBPTS certification. At the conclusion of the seminar, teachers will be in a better position to make an informed decision about their readiness to become candidates.

The seminar is structured to place strong emphasis on the five NBPTS core propositions and the standards for each certificate field. Furthermore, it enables potential candidates to participate in activities that simulate the NBPTS assessment process of preparing a school-site portfolio and responding to an assessment center prompt (question or activity). The seminar also allows participants to engage in exercises that foster reflective practice using their current teaching setting as a resource.

Our work with candidates has shown us that those who take the time to fully reflect upon their teaching, while keeping the NBPTS propositions and standards in mind, develop a deeper sense of the total NBPTS assessment process. In contrast, those who dismiss the propositions and standards as unimportant ultimately find themselves either returning to them or producing written responses that lack the depth required to achieve certification.

As the number of available certificates increases, the core propositions and standards, which are the connective threads that tie all the certificates together and relate to the NBPTS mission, will become an even more essential component of candidate success that the facilitators must also bear in mind.

This chapter provides an outline for an introductory seminar to inform teachers about the NBPTS assessment process. The activities and exercises described below may be easily adapted to accommodate the participants regardless of their certification field or the size of the group. The introductory seminar consists of five three-hour sessions held once a week over a five-week period. (A three- to six-hour abbreviated version of the seminar is described in Appendix 3.2.) Each session is outlined for quick reference; the outline includes objectives and an agenda. These are followed by detailed descriptions of activities, based on the facilitators' actual experiences. A Resources list for seminar facilitators is included, as is a list of the materials needed for each session including masters of the overheads (see Appendix 3.1). Two resources are recommended to complement this seminar:

- The materials distributed by the NBPTS, which provide an overview of the NBPTS and its assessment process (*What Every Teacher Should Know: The National Board Certification Process Q & A, 1999–2000*).
- The portfolio samplers available for Generalist, Early adolescence, Adolescence and young adulthood fields, which describe the certification fields available each year.

Sessions should be advertised in advance. The sessions should be held after school hours at a convenient, central location. The seminar facilitator should read all NBPTS materials before presenting, and if possible, should also consider co-facilitating with an NBCT.

SEMINAR SESSION 1

Objectives

The participant will:

- Gain an overview of the NBPTS process.
- Be introduced to the art of reflective practice.

- Examine the five core propositions of the NBPTS.
- Have the opportunity to ask questions.

(Overhead 1)

Agenda

- Welcome/opening remarks
- Writing prompt
- Overview of the NBPTS
- The five core propositions
- Creating a core proposition web
- Questions and answers
- Closing remarks/handouts (Summary of Standards)

(Overhead 2)

Each agenda item is detailed below.

Welcome/Opening Remarks

The session facilitators introduce themselves, highlighting their experience with the NBPTS. They then ask the candidate participants to introduce themselves and include a brief description of where they teach, the grade level of their students, and the reasons for their interest in the NBPTS. The participants' introductory remarks will enable the facilitators to determine how much knowledge the participants have about the NBPTS process.

During the introductions seminar facilitators need to note the probable fields of certification and the grade levels of the teachers. This information will assist them in creating collaborative groups.

Facilitators should distribute a form for participants to complete that will ask for name, work and home phone numbers, school name and location, e-mail address, and the field of certification being pursued. Facilitators can use individual lists to create a master list to distribute to all members of the seminar to encourage collaboration. Facilitators should also establish a help-line to answer questions that may arise during the seminar.

Writing Prompt

The next step is to model the stages that the NBPTS itself went through as it developed the certification process. To do this, seminar facilitators ask participants to respond individually to a writing prompt displayed via an overhead transparency or a chart. This activity will also lead teachers into the practice of reflection.

(Overhead 3)

Allow the participants plenty of time to respond. Observe the group's progress to determine if they need more time. Then ask participants to share their individual responses with the group. Create a chart listing the various characteristics mentioned as a point of reference for further discussion. If the group is large, facilitators may want to break into smaller groups to identify attributes and then share the smaller groups' work with all the participants.

Responses will probably include some of the following characteristics:

- Good listener
- Enthusiastic and excited about teaching
- Cared about the students
- Made learning fun and interesting
- Challenged the students in the classroom
- Actively involved with their students
- Fair and unbiased
- Set high expectations
- Knew their subjects
- Creative
- Good storytellers

Once you have recorded the attributes of the memorable teachers, ask participants to note any connections between their list of characteristics and the propositions developed by the NBPTS.

(Overhead 4)

For example, the list above indicates that outstanding teachers "cared about the students" and were "fair and unbiased." These statements are directly connected to the NBPTS's first proposition, "Teachers are committed to students and their learning." This proposition states that teachers "treat students equitably, recognizing the individual differences that distinguish their students from one another."

Explain to your group that this is the very process that the NBPTS used to develop its core propositions and to define what constitutes excellent teaching practice. It is important for the participants to understand that the process involved in the development of the core propositions and standards is similar to the activity in which they have just participated. Also, underscore the fact that the NBPTS, while in the initial process of developing each certification field, directly involved teachers in setting its standards, which are guided by the core propositions.

Overview of the NBPTS

During this activity participants gain more knowledge about the NBPTS process and how it applies to their own teaching practice. Several sources have created quality videotapes expressly for seminar facilitators to use to introduce potential candidates to the NBPTS assessment process. (See the Resources list for suggestions and information on ordering.) Following screening of a selected videotape, facilitators should invite questions and take the time to stress the positive impact of the NBPTS on the teaching profession.

Along with the overheads used here, the NBPTS also provides materials for facilitators. The *National Board Faculty Meeting Kit* (NBPTS, 1997) is regularly updated to include the most recent information about the NBPTS. The *Meeting Kit* includes a complete overview of the NBPTS process, a history of the NBPTS's progress, and a breakdown of the many levels of national, state, and local support. By combining the overheads and talking points, facilitators may choose the most applicable information to present to the group.

The Five Core Propositions

This activity uses a collaborative approach to examine the key elements of the core propositions. The facilitators should divide participants into five small groups, and assign each group one of the core propositions. Instruct the individuals within each group to carefully read the description of their designated core proposition and highlight its salient points with a marker. Within each group, ask one participant to share one of his or her underlined points, without making any comment about the choice. Ask the other participants in the group to comment on their interpretation of that sentence (or pass if they wish). After each group member has had an opportunity to respond, ask the individual who underlined the sentence to explain why he or she highlighted it. This procedure continues around the group until each member has had a chance to read an underlined sentence, receive group comment, and explain his or her choice.

Creating a Core Proposition Web

Ask each group to create a web of classroom activities that illustrates the proposition they have just discussed. Then have each group share their webs with the other small groups in order to provide a visual image of the connection between the core propositions and real teaching practices. For example, a web for Proposition 3, "Teachers are responsible for managing and monitoring student learning," might include the following items: student–teacher conferences, anecdotal records, student self-assessments, rubrics, preassessment of student knowledge and learning, journal responses, and tests and quizzes.

Questions and Answers

Encourage participants to ask questions. Keep in mind that the majority of participants who attend the first session will have many questions. NBPTS literature answers most of the questions participants might ask. Facilitators should be familiar with this literature. Certainly, however, participants will ask questions the facilitators will be unable to answer. Write these questions down and contact the NBPTS for answers. Then, at the beginning of the next seminar session, share the NBPTS's answers with the group. Some of the questions that frequently arise include:

- How do I apply?
- What assistance and support do local districts, the state, or professional organizations offer?
- How many hours will the process take?
- What type of student work samples should I be keeping? (The NBPTS application and portfolios provide some examples.)
- Who scores the assessments?
- How long is the certificate valid?

Time for a question-and-answer period should be built into each session. Not only does this encourage dialogue, it also assists in the creation of a comfort zone for those who are new to the NBPTS process.

Closing Remarks/Handouts (Summary of Standards)

Ask participants to do some reading before the next seminar session (usually scheduled for the following week). This will provide them with additional information and allow them to "try out" some of the NBPTS activities.

ASSIGNMENT 1

At the end of the session, distribute the overview page(s) of the standards for the potential certification fields of the participants. (These are available from the NBPTS by calling 1-800-22-TEACH and requesting standards books.) Ask the teachers to reflect upon the standards for their certificate field and to list two or three teaching practices that they are currently implementing that might address each standard.

ASSIGNMENT 2

Ask participants who have access to the necessary equipment to videotape a 5- to 10-minute segment from their current teaching practice. Emphasize that the tape will be used only for the purpose of identifying standards in practice and will not be evaluated or used outside the seminar. This exercise will help to introduce the process of self-evaluation and reflection, as well as the videotaping process.

SEMINAR SESSION 2

Objectives

The participants will:

- Identify teaching practices that demonstrate the standards.
- Highlight standards reflected in a commentary on a student's writing and in video vignettes of classroom practice.
- Gain an overview of the portfolio requirements.

(Overhead 5)

Agenda

- Sharing homework responses
- Identifying standards in portfolio samples
- Documenting accomplished practice
- Professional reading
- Questions and answers
- Individual conferencing

(Overhead 6)

Sharing Homework Responses

Session 2 begins with participants discussing their written assignments, in which they identified samples of the standards in their own practice. This allows all participants the opportunity to hear the similarities and major themes that are emphasized in each certification field. Facilitators should encourage participants to make connections between these responses and the five core propositions. These connections serve as an introduction to the next segment of the seminar: an overview of the importance of the standards. Examples drawn from the standards for a Middle Childhood/Generalist follow. For example,

> Standard I in Middle Childhood/Generalist says: *Accomplished teachers draw on their knowledge of child development and their relationships with their students to understand their students' abilities, interests, aspirations, and values.*
>
> A teacher might link this standard to classroom practice in the following way. Before beginning a unit on the Civil War, the teacher passed out an "interest inventory" asking the students about specific interests in relation to the upcoming study. Categories in the inventory included art, poetry, music, battles and strategies, people, photography, and news events. These areas of interest were used to create student assignments that complemented their Civil War studies.
>
> Standard IV says: *Accomplished teachers help students learn to respect individual and group differences in the following manner.*
>
> The teacher might share how he or she has implemented a peer mediation program to resolve student conflicts. In that setting, students listen to and respect differing viewpoints as they work out a mutually acceptable solution.

Identifying Standards in Portfolio Samples

For this exercise facilitators will need to purchase the NBPTS portfolio sampler (see Resources at the end of this chapter). Distribute sample copies of the standards booklets from which the summaries for the previous session were copied.

Allow time for the candidates to skim through copies of the standards booklets and compare them to the standards summary pages distributed during the previous session (see Assignment 1). Divide participants into groups by field of certification and give each group one teacher narrative that provides evidence of the standards in practice (see Appendix 5.2, in Chapter 5.) Assign each participant the task of identifying specific standards for which evidence is found in the teachers' narratives. After giving participants sufficient time to scan the narratives and standards, ask each teacher to share his or her findings with the group. Each group should then be prepared to offer three summary statements about the NBPTS assessment process learned through this experience.

Here are some examples of possible responses:

- "It helps to give me a more global view of my teaching. This helps me to think about what I am doing that is good and what areas I need to work on."
- "It makes you question why you're doing what you're doing and how it is 'best practice' for students."
- "Whenever there are established criteria, an individual has the opportunity to judge his or her own practice against those criteria. This gives one the opportunity to find the strengths in one's teaching and to develop in areas of need."

The next step to identifying standards in practice is to use the videotapes brought in by participants (which will probably represent a variety of certificate fields). Such a discussion allows participants to (1) find and discuss examples of specific standards demonstrated in the tapes, and (2) practice making distinctions between describing, analyzing, and reflecting.

Participants can be asked to cite specific standards that they observe in the videotapes and to explain their choices. This step in video analysis is very important.

It is critical that participants recognize the crucial differences between describing, analyzing, and reflecting when discussing their teaching practice. Using an example from the video, the facilitator should ask a participant to describe what the teacher in the videotape is doing. The facilitator should write this response on a chart headed "Description." Next, the facilitator should ask another participant to explain how the behavior is connected to student learning. Write this response on another chart titled "Analysis." Finally, the facilitator should ask the teacher who videotaped this segment to share why he or she chose this particular portion of a lesson to tape, how he or she believes the instructional goals were achieved, and whether or not he or she would consider making any changes in the future. Write this response on a third chart labeled "Reflection."

Point out that the three responses illustrate the different types of writing that the NBPTS expects and requires as a candidate moves through the NBPTS process. Be sure that prospective candidates understand that they will need to explain "what" they are doing in their classrooms, but even more important they must be able to fully document "why" they are using particular teaching practices and "how" these practices impact student learning.

Documenting Accomplished Practice

By this point in the seminar participants are usually eager to get a glimpse of the portfolio entries for their respective certification fields. Facilitators may obtain portfolio samples by contacting the NBPTS.

Two portfolio entries are common to all certification areas: Entry 5, Documented Accomplishments I, which demonstrates the teacher's collaborative activities in the professional community, and Entry 6, Documented Accomplishments II, which focuses on a teacher's outreach to student families and the community. By asking participants to reflect upon and document their professional development and service, session facilitators can help potential candidates begin to think about these entries. In both Entries 5 and 6, teachers are required to select specific activities and accomplishments that will illustrate their commitment to their colleagues and to the families and communities of the students whom they teach. Accomplished teachers see themselves as members of a community of learners that includes other educators, students, their families, and the community at large. Understanding the power of collaboration, they engage in numerous activities that will extend the support and assistance necessary to ensure the success of all students.

Documented accomplishments might include activities such as a professional development session that the teacher conducted to share an effective teaching strategy or a presentation at a state or national conference. Outreach to families and the community could include activities such as organizing a family math night, conducting parent conferences, or setting up a speaker program using community volunteers. (Extensive examples of accomplishments are provided in Chapters 4–7.)

Through their documented accomplishments, teachers provide evidence that they have stepped outside the boundaries of their classroom and taken an active role in their school and local community.

Copies of the Documented Accomplishments I entry should be made available to each participant. Facilitators should work through the directions and requirements for this particular exercise because the process for this entry serves as a model, regardless of certification field, for approaching all the entries. Each participant should locate in the standards document the standards that correspond to the professional community.

ACTIVITY

The following jigsaw strategy fosters total group comprehension of this entry.

- Divide participants into four groups.
- Assign each group a number, 1 through 4, to work on the separate sections of the entry:

  Group 1 Sections: "What is the nature of this entry?," "What do I need to do?," "How will my response be scored?," and the summary of the entry.
  Group 2 Section: "Making good choices"
  Group 3 Section: "Preparing your documentation."
  Group 4 Section: "Writing your description and interpretive summary."

- Assign each group the task of reading its respective segment of the entry so that all members can discuss the relevant information and create a summary. Make it clear to the participants that each member will be required to teach this segment to the three other groups, emphasizing the key points.
- Once each group has completed its initial assignments, rotate all group members so that there is at least one representative from Groups 1 through 4 present in each new group arrangement. The newly formed groups begin with a Group 1 member who explains what the first section on Background entails. A Group 2 member follows. This process continues until all sections of Entries 5 and 6 have been introduced within each of the newly formed groups.
- Once all groups have been introduced to each section of Entries 5 and 6, the facilitator should provide participants with chart paper to brainstorm examples of what types of personal experiences, professional development activities, and participant involvement would be suitable to document accomplished practice. The brainstormed list will become useful to the participants, who will be required to make appropriate choices for their individual responses. It will also prepare them for the assignment following this session.

SAMPLE RESPONSES

- Teacher was a member of a committee that developed and helped to implement the school plan.
- Teacher developed and facilitated the implementation of a schoolwide character education program.
- Teacher published an article in a professional journal.
- Teacher presented a paper or an instructional strategy at a local, state, or national conference.

Professional Reading

Distribute copies of a selected professional reading (see the Resources list at the end of this chapter and Chapters 4–7 for suggestions). Allow ample time for the participants to read the document. Then conduct a large-group discussion based on the professional reading selection. Ask participants the kinds of questions that will allow them to connect the selected reading to accomplished teaching practice. Three to four prepared, open-ended questions should generate professional dialogue. This dialogue will be useful in the preparation of future portfolio entries when candidates reflect on their own teaching practice.

For example, ask participants to read David Elkind's (1989) "Developmentally Appropriate Practice: Philosophical and Practical Implications." Good follow-up questions could include: What did you read that could be applied to your own teaching practice? What connections could be made between the article and the core propositions of the NBPTS?

Questions and Answers/Individual Conferencing

Allow time for participants in each certification field to preview the portfolio requirements for their respective fields. While the participants are previewing the portfolios, facilitators should conduct individual conferences to answer any questions that interested participants may have.

ASSIGNMENT 3

Create your own list of professional development accomplishments and services to your school, community, and profession. Identify artifacts and documents that support your list, for example, a flyer created and sent out to parents to notify them of a schoolwide event that you helped organize; letters from supervisors thanking or commending you for work you have done on schoolwide or systemwide committees; a certificate you received after presenting a workshop; or a copy of an article that you published.

SEMINAR SESSION 3

Objectives

The participants will:

- Increase their awareness of the portfolio requirements.
- Learn tips on using a video camera.
- Become members of a support group.

(Overhead 7)

Agenda

- Peer conferences
- Hands-on videotaping workshop
- Thematic exploration/interdisciplinary connections
- Portfolio preview
- Questions and answers
- Individual conferencing

(Overhead 8)

Peer Conferences

Working with partners, candidates share the professional accomplishments they documented in their last assignment and identify the standards that apply to them. Facilitators encourage them to add to their own lists as they listen to their peers' lists. This sharing process may help them to think of additional items that they may have overlooked or forgotten to mention.

Through peer conferences, candidates begin to experience the importance of having "critical friends," a necessary component of the assessment process. Facilitators encourage participants to provide each other with feedback and request clarification if needed. The facilitator then asks them to return to the large-group setting. Each participant shares one accomplishment from his or her list, states what impact it had on his or her professional growth, and explains how it strengthened his or her commitment to the teaching profession. This activity serves the dual purpose of connecting standards to personal experience and promoting collaboration among potential candidates.

Hands-On Videotaping Workshop

Facilitators should invite a school media specialist or someone else who has expert knowledge of videotaping to present tips to candidates on videotaping classroom activities for the portfolio. Some school systems may have a media center whose director could provide this kind of information, but anyone knowledgeable about the use of video equipment could be of great assistance. The video expert should go over essential elements of a successful taping experience and discuss available resources that a candidate may find helpful. Facilitators themselves should review the Videotaping: Technical Aspects and Videotaping: Analysis hints in the Introduction to Part II of this book.

The facilitator should emphasize two points: the videos are to be used as evidence to support participants' written portfolio entries, and the videos' assessors should be able to see the standards in practice in the candidates' classrooms. One teacher noted:

> "Having to tape myself and actually reflect on it will help me answer some questions I need answered: How fast do I talk? What levels of questions dominate my teaching? How can I communicate better with children for whom English is not their native language? Where am I missing inquiry questions?"

Provide plenty of time for a question-and-answer session with the video expert, as many candidates are anxious about videotaping. Possible questions to expect include:

- How can I instruct and tape at the same time?
- Can students do the taping for me?
- How professional should the taping be?
- How can I make sure all student voices will be heard?
- Should I make copies?
- How many students should be in each segment?

Thematic Explorations/Interdisciplinary Connections

Many of the portfolio entries require demonstration of interdisciplinary connections. The facilitator should ask all participants to brainstorm a list of concepts that could be developed for a unit of study in science—for example, patterns, systems, connections, and change are concepts that lend themselves naturally to interdisciplinary teaching. Once the list is created, the facilitator should divide participants into groups, and assign each group one concept to explore. Each group then creates a list of generalizations that could be applied to that concept. These generalizations are then linked to other disciplines.

Sample: Concept and Generalizations: Systems

1. Generalizations
   - Systems have elements that can be listed and defined.
   - Elements in a system are interconnected.
   - Systems have limits both externally and internally.
   - Systems exist within systems.
2. Interdisciplinary connections
   - government systems
   - ecosystems
   - mathematical systems (equations)
   - economic systems
   - elements of a story make up a system

Distribute to each participant the requirements of a sample portfolio entry from a NBPTS portfolio that pertains to thematic/interdisciplinary teaching. Using the directions for the selected entry as a guide, have participants work in small groups to select a concept or theme that could be developed for this entry. (See Chapters 4, 5, 6, and 7 for additional examples.)

Questions and Answers/Individual Conferencing

Provide time for questions and answers as well as individual conferences as needed.

ASSIGNMENT 4

Facilitators lead a discussion about how differentiated instruction meets specific learner needs and chart what some of those needs might be. These might include students' learning style, interests, developmental level, ability level, special needs (such as English as a second language and learning disabilities), and family background. Facilitators encourage participants to choose one or more students and write about these students in a journal using *descriptive*, *analytical*, and *reflective* writing (discussed in Session 2). Facilitators also ask them to collect work samples, assignments, and any other evidence that could be used to provide evidence of how they met specific needs.

ASSIGNMENT 5

Read a professional article pertaining to a topic found in the standards booklet (e.g., a recent article on the debate about whole-language or developmentally appropriate [DAP] literacy). Bring in copies of the article for other participants to review and be prepared to give a brief overview of the article and the reason for your choice.

SEMINAR SESSION 4

Objectives

The participants will:

- Clearly define the components of a case study.
- Discuss their individual progress on the creation of student profiles.
- Further investigate descriptive, analytical, and reflective writing practices as they apply to the portfolio process.
- Respond to a writing prompt simulating an assessment center activity.

(Overhead 9)

Agenda

- Professional dialogue
- Develop a student case study
- Assessment center prompt
- Questions and answers
- Individual conferencing

(Overhead 10)

Professional Dialogue

Begin Session 4 by asking candidates to briefly (2–3 minutes) share the key components of their self-selected article. Each candidate should distribute copies of the article to all members of the group prior to sharing. The articles can serve as an excellent professional resource not only for the completion of the NBPTS assessment process, but also as a vehicle to encourage professional thought and dialogue. Allow time for all participants to share.

Develop a Student Case Study

Accomplished teachers are able to identify specific learner needs and then to design instruction that is differentiated in order to meet those needs. By using a case study to track a student during a particular unit of study, a candidate is able to share the multiple paths to learning that are created in his or her classroom and demonstrate the direct impact they have on improving student achievement. The number of students, the time the case study covers, and the specified work samples required differ for each certification field. However, the purpose across all fields remains the same: to provide concrete evidence that the teacher is able to differentiate instruction in response to the unique characteristics of individual learners.

Facilitators distribute copies of sample student case studies. (These can be extracted from teacher narratives and sample responses in Chapters 4, 5, 6, and 7.) These should represent a variety of developmental levels to satisfy all fields of certification represented by the seminar participants. Allow enough time for participants to identify individually at least three components of a case study that are critical to the evaluation of a student's progress.

Once all candidates have identified components of a case study, facilitators should request examples from the group and list responses on chart paper. This process will highlight the important characteristics that participants should consider as they select students for future portfolio requirements. These may include such areas as age of student (developmental and chronological), gender, special needs and characteristics, family background, learning style, primary language spoken in the home, or academic strengths and weaknesses.

For the next step, the facilitator should challenge participants to take a descriptive observation from a case study that they read and extend it through an analytical or reflective comment. An example is given below. This process reemphasizes to group members the importance of the three types of writing required in many of the portfolio entries—descriptive, analytical, and reflective—and how these can be applied to a case study. Ask participants to identify specific learner needs and explain how they would tailor instruction to address those needs.

Examples for Participants

1. Descriptive comment from a case study: John is an auditory learner who often does not complete assignments and seems unsure of what to do when he is expected to follow through on a set of written instructions.
2. Analytical response: Because John needs to hear the written word, the teacher changed the way she presented information and made sure that all directions were read out loud before the students were expected to proceed with an assignment.
3. Reflective response: The teacher noticed that with this adaptation in place, John was more successful in completing assignments and needed to ask fewer clarifying questions.

Assessment Center Prompt

This segment of Session 4 requires facilitators to investigate the requirements for the assessment center activities for each certification field. Before candidates participate in the assessment center during the last part of the assessment process, the NBPTS sends them information explaining how they should prepare. (Samples of assessment center activities can be found in Chapters 4, 5, 6, and 7.)

Once the facilitators identify specific expectations, they should create a writing prompt that will simulate an assessment center exercise. This provides the participants with the opportunity to practice applying their knowledge of content and pedagogy into an instructional unit or strategy. The facilitators should collect the responses for review in order to provide feedback at the next session.

Questions and Answers/Individual Conferencing

Give the participants the opportunity to ask final questions and speak individually with the facilitators.

ASSIGNMENT 6

Prepare one student profile (case study) for a final presentation. This assignment provides potential candidates the opportunity to further examine the work of one of their students by collecting work samples. Participants will be asked to present an analysis of the student's work at the next session. (Parent permission may be required for this assignment. Check on local school policy regarding use of student work.)

SEMINAR SESSION 5

Objectives

The participant will:

- Receive feedback on assessment center writing and their student profiles.
- Have the opportunity for final reflection and collaboration.
- Finalize support network system.

(Overhead 11)

Agenda

- Feedback for writing prompts
- Student profile presentations
- Conclusion of seminar

(Overhead 12)

Feedback for Writing Prompts

Begin Session 5 by distributing the written responses to the assessment center prompt from Session 4. Allow time for questions. It is important to provide immediate feedback to the participants.

Student Profile Presentations

Turn the class over to the participants, who will now present their individual student profiles. Allow plenty of time for each presentation and for follow-up comments or questions from the group. Consider the amount of time available for the session and the number of candidates presenting to determine the length of each presentation. We recommend three to five minutes for each presentation and five to eight minutes for follow-up comments and/or questions.

Conclusion of Seminar

Participants should have a final opportunity to ask questions regarding the NBPTS process. Session 5 should bring the seminar to an end on a positive note of reassurance and allow the opportunity for last thoughts and reflections. During this last session facilitators should ask for input from the participants regarding the effectiveness of the seminar and solicit suggestions for improving future seminars.

If participants have decided to apply for NBPTS certification, it is essential to establish a successful networking program for them to receive continual support and feedback. This support may be provided in a number of different ways. In some areas, continued support may be provided through a collaborative effort with a university staff development program or with NBCTs in the school system. Chapter 2 delineates a collaborative support process that provides timelines, meeting dates, and resources facilitators can use to develop support during the Candidacy phase.

CONCLUSION

The process of becoming an NBCT is more than an assessment process. It is an opportunity for professional growth and development that encourages participants to reflect upon what constitutes accomplished teaching practices. The NBPTS experience requires teachers to critically examine their own practices in order to identify their strengths and build upon the effectiveness of these strengths. It is based upon real-life practice and is immediately applicable to a candidate's teaching. An increase in the number of NBPTS teachers who share a common vision and mission will provide our nation with more effective curriculum implementation, stronger professional standards, and greater achievement by students.

It is important for the facilitators of an NBPTS pre-candidacy support seminar to deliver the message of professional growth as an integral part of the process. The benefits of completing the process regardless of final achievement warrant consideration and support. In order for the process to have a major impact, however, an ongoing support network is critical. The walls of isolation are best broken down by building a cadre of professionals who seek to achieve the shared goals outlined in the NBPTS mission statement and core propositions. Establishing high standards for the teaching professional also makes it possible to ensure that our students achieve more, knowing that the decision maker in the classroom has volunteered to take the steps necessary to define accomplished practice. Support seminars play an integral role in maintaining the integrity of the process and in ensuring that the NBPTS mission is clearly understood.

RESOURCES

NBPTS Materials

The following items may be ordered from the National Board for Professional Teaching Standards by phone at 1-800-22-TEACH or by mail to NBPTS c/o AFFINA, 800 Kirts, Suite 600, Troy, MI 48084.

> *National Board Faculty Meeting Kit* (includes video: *Something Is Happening across America*, $25)
> *What Every Teacher Should Know about the Board Process Q&A, 1999–2000* (first copy free; charge for quantity orders)
> *What Teachers Should Know and Be Able to Do* ($5)
> Videotape: *National Board Certification: Something That Furthers Your Love of Teaching and Learning* ($10)

The following can be ordered by calling 1-800-211-8378.

> *Adolescence and Young Adulthood Portfolio Sampler* ($40)
> *Early Adolescence Portfolio Sampler* ($40)
> *Generalist Portfolio Sampler* ($40)
> *National Board Standards Booklets* ($15 per booklet). A booklet is available for each certification field. Each includes a detailed explanation of accomplished practice for that field.

Professional Readings

Berk, L. (1997). *Child development*. Boston: Allyn & Bacon
Brandt, R. (1998). *Powerful learning*. Alexandria, VA: Association for Supervision and Curriculum Development.

Danielson, C. (1996). *Enhancing professional practice: A framework for teaching.* Alexandria, VA: Association for Supervision and Curriculum Development.

Darling-Hammond, L., & Falk, B. (1998, November). Using standards and assessments to support student learning. *Phi Delta Kappan, 79*(3), 190–199.

Elkind, D. (1989, October). Developmentally appropriate practice: Philosophical and practical implications. *Phi Delta Kappan, 71*(2), 113–117.

Erickson, H. L. (1998). *Concept-based curriculum and instruction.* Thousand Oaks, CA: Corwin Press.

Harlen, W. (1985). *Primary science: Taking the plunge.* Portsmouth, NH: Heinemann.

Junn, E. (Ed.). (1999). *Annual editions: Child growth and development, 1999–2000.* Sluice Dock, CT: Dushkin/McGraw-Hill.

Strachota, B. (1996). *On their side: Helping children take charge of their learning.* Greenfield, ME: Northeast Foundation for Children.

Tomlinson, C. (1999). *The differentiated classroom: Responding to the needs of all learners.* Alexandria, VA: Association for Supervision and Curriculum Development.

Wiggins, G., & McTighe, J. (1998). *Understanding by design.* Alexandria, VA: Association for Supervision and Curriculum Development.

Wiggins, G., & McTighe, J. (1999). *Understanding by design handbook.* Alexandria, VA: Association for Supervision and Curriculum Development.

APPENDIX 3.1
Materials Facilitators Need for Seminar Sessions

The following are materials needed for all sessions: chart paper, index cards, pencils, markers, highlighters, overhead projector, VCR, and television.

Session 1

Refreshments
Information form
Writing prompt (Overhead 3)
NBPTS introductory video, *Something Is Happening across America*
NBPTS Talking Points from National Board Faculty Meeting Kit
Core propositions
NBPTS video for session summary
Standards overview (summary pages for each certificate field)

Session 2

Selected portfolio samples and video clips
Standards booklets (for certificate fields represented by group)
Copies of Portfolio Entry 5, Documented Accomplishments I
Facilitator-selected professional reading

Session 3

Video clips prepared by class members (Assignment 2)
Copies of the NBPTS materials on videotaping (found in Part II of this book)
Focus lesson materials on concept-/theme-based instruction. A sample application to science follows, in Appendix 3.3

Session 4

Participants' (and/or facilitators) self-selected professional reading
Copies of several student case studies (see Chapter 5, Appendix 5.2, and Chapter 6, Appendix 6.1)
Assessment center prompts (for each certificate field represented by group)

Session 5

Student case studies (prepared by participants)

Overheads

Overhead 1: Session 1 Objectives
Overhead 2: Session 1 Agenda
Overhead 3: Session 1 Writing Prompt
Overhead 4: Core Propositions
Overhead 5: Session 2 Objectives
Overhead 6: Session 2 Agenda
Overhead 7: Session 3 Objectives
Overhead 8: Session 3 Agenda
Overhead 9: Session 4 Objectives
Overhead 10: Session 4 Agenda
Overhead 11: Session 5 Objectives
Overhead 12: Session 5 Agenda

OVERHEAD 1.
SESSION 1 OBJECTIVES

The participants will:

- Gain an overview of the NBPTS process.

- Practice the art of reflective practice.

- Examine the five core propositions of the NBPTS.

- Have the opportunity to ask questions.

OVERHEAD 2.
SESSION 1 AGENDA

Welcome/Opening Remarks

Writing Prompt

Overview of the NBPTS

The Five Core Propositions

Creating a Core Proposition Web

Questions and Answers

Closing Remarks/Handout (Summary of Standards)

OVERHEAD 3.
SESSION 1 WRITING PROMPT

Write a brief description of a teacher you
remember positively from your experience
as a student.

List the characteristics you believe made
that teacher so effective.

OVERHEAD 4.
FIVE CORE PROPOSITIONS

Teachers are committed to students and their learning.

Teachers know the subjects they teach and how to teach those subjects to students.

Teachers are responsible for managing and monitoring student learning.

Teachers think systematically about their practice and learn from experience.

Teachers are members of learning communities.

OVERHEAD 5.
SESSION 2 OBJECTIVES

The participants will:

- Identify teaching practices that demonstrate the standards.

- Highlight standards reflected in a commentary on a student's writing and in video vignettes of classroom practice.

- Gain an overview of the portfolio requirements.

OVERHEAD 6.
SESSION 2 AGENDA

Sharing Homework Responses

Identifying Standards in Portfolio Samples

Documenting Accomplished Practice

Professional Reading

Questions and Answers

Individual Conferencing

OVERHEAD 7.
SESSION 3 OBJECTIVES

The participants will:

- Increase their awareness of the portfolio requirements.

- Learn tips on using a video camera.

- Become members of a support group.

OVERHEAD 8.
SESSION 3 AGENDA

Peer Conferences

Hands-on Videotaping Workshop

Thematic Exploration/Interdisciplinary Connections

Portfolio Preview

Questions and Answers

Individual Conferencing

OVERHEAD 9.
SESSION 4 OBJECTIVES

The participants will:

- Clearly define the components of a case study.

- Discuss individual progress on the creation of student profiles.

- Further investigate descriptive, analytical, and reflective writing practices as they apply to the portfolio process.

- Respond to a writing prompt simulating an assessment center activity.

OVERHEAD 10.
SESSION 4 AGENDA

Professional Dialogue

Develop a Student Case Study

Assessment Center Prompt

Questions and Answers

Individual Conferencing

OVERHEAD 11.
SESSION 5 OBJECTIVES

The participants will:

- Receive feedback on assessment center writing and their student profiles.

- Have the opportunity for final reflection and collaboration.

- Finalize support system network.

OVERHEAD 12.
SESSION 5 AGENDA

Feedback on Writing Prompts

Student Profile Presentations

Conclusion of Seminar

APPENDIX 3.2
Three- to Six-Hour Version of Seminar

This shortened version of the full introductory seminar attempts to give the participants necessary background on the NBPTS and an overview of the assessment process, concentrating on the core propositions and the standards. Unlike the full seminar with its five-session structure, the mini-seminar does not try to provide the participants with simulations of the assessment pieces. The following sections of the full seminar are recommended as a base to develop a three- to six-hour seminar.

From Session 1

- Writing Prompt
- Overview of the NBPTS
- The Five Core Propositions
- Creating a Core Proposition Web (if time allows)
- Assignment 1: Videotape current teaching practice

From Session 2

- Documenting Accomplished Practice. (If time does not allow using the jigsaw activity, have participants think about their own accomplishments, share this information with a partner, and then share with the entire group. The results of the sharing will stimulate recollections of similar experiences.)

From Session 3

- Hands-on Videotaping Workshop
- Thematic Explorations/Interdisciplinary Connections (Use exercise at the end if time allows.)

From Session 4

- Developing a Student Case Study (Use exercises as time allows.)
- Assessment Center Prompt (Use only the first paragraph.)

In addition, session facilitators need to emphasize the value of support groups as candidates experience the assessment process. They also need to review the professional benefits of going through the NBPTS assessment process.

APPENDIX 3.3
Sample Science Application

The program of studies for general education science classes incorporates a unit on *body systems*. A lesson might require a student to "investigate and understand that organisms perform life processes that are essential to survive and perpetuate the species."

Overview

The students will gain an understanding of the human body as a complex network of systems within systems, interconnected and interdependent. By learning and applying the general principles that govern all systems, the students will better understand the inner workings of the human body system. The students will learn to identify the *elements, input, output, boundaries,* and *connections* of each of the systems in the human body, beginning with one of the smallest systems, the living cell. As they recognize how the different systems are connected and how they interact, they will also gain an appreciation for the necessity of keeping all systems in a healthy state. This will lead to a comprehension of their responsibility to make the choices in life that will impact their body systems in a positive way. As they gain an understanding of the connection between a healthy body and their choices, they will understand the meaning of a healthy lifestyle, and they will be better able to defend the reasoning behind making healthy choices.

Key Concept: Systems

Students will gain an understanding of the concept of *systems* and the basic principles governing all systems. They will understand how the properties and interactions of individual parts of a system affect the overall behavior of a system. It will deepen their understanding of the world around them as they recognize the many complex systems of the world in which we live and the variables that affect these systems both positively and negatively.

System definition: A collection of identifiable elements and processes that interact with each other and interconnect to create a definable unit. All systems have the following properties (generalizations):

1. They are made up of identifiable elements that interact with each other and respond to input from outside sources.
2. They require balance to be healthy.
3. There are systems within systems and they are interconnected.
4. Each element of a system has a unique and important role to play.
5. Systems have boundaries.
6. Systems receive input from outside of their boundaries, and generate output.

PART TWO

Candidacy

INTRODUCTION

Part II contains four chapters that provide guidance for the facilitator working with teachers preparing their portfolios for submission to the NBPTS. Each chapter focuses on a specific certification field and is written by National Board Certified Teachers (NBCTs) who have earned that particular certificate.

The format for all the chapters is the same. The Certification Characteristics section introduces the requirements for the chosen certification field. This is followed by a Standards section that explains the standards for each field. A General Hints section offers helpful ideas for facilitators. A Certification Field Organizer section then provides an advance organizer to address each entry. While each chapter has the same format, the information in each chapter applies to the specific certificate the chapter addresses. A blank field organizer, included in Chapter 4, Figure 4.2, can be used by facilitators as they work with additional certification fields.

Each chapter presents information regarding all six entries required in the NBPTS portfolio. Each entry includes a general description, the standards addressed, hints for facilitators, activities to assist candidates, and a resource list. A final section of each chapter addresses the assessment center activities for that certification. As part of this overview, we include a compilation of hints based on the experiences of all of the authors. This list of hints is divided into the following sections:

- General
- Getting Started
- Standards
- Portfolio
- Videotaping: Technical Aspects
- Videotaping: Analysis
- Reflective Practice
- Written Commentary
- Developing a Student Case Study
- Finishing the Portfolio
- Assessment Center

Our book provides information about two generalist and two content-specific certification fields. They can be used as a "blueprint" (guide) to help facilitators expand their support of NBPTS candidates into other areas of certification.

We should note that some of the activities from the generalist chapters (Chapters 4 and 5) may be useful in the specific certificate fields (Chapters 6 and 7). For example, some of the activities suggested in the Early Adolescence/Generalist (EA/G) chapter address mathematics. Those activities may prove useful in work with candidates in Adolescence/Young Adulthood/Mathematics (AYA/M), since the age ranges and the content overlap. Other such connections will be noted as they come up in their respective chapters.

Within the Activities section and in the Appendices of each chapter, sample entries are included as examples of possible responses to NBPTS portfolio entries. They are intended for practice use and do not represent actual entries.

HINTS

General

- Candidates should be constantly reminded that many styles and structures of teaching can be appropriate and successful. Because the NBPTS does not advocate any particular teaching style, teachers should relax and "be themselves."

- Remind candidates that they are supposed to demonstrate what normally happens in their classrooms, not some extraordinary event.

- Call the NBPTS as many times as you want to ask questions. Directions can be ambiguous, leading to multiple interpretations. Make sure you understand what the NBPTS expects so you can help the candidates understand what they need to do.

- The facilitator is an important source of encouragement when the candidates face time crunches. Remind them of their strengths and point out that the certification process is really nothing more than a documentation of what they already do well.

- Encourage candidates to conduct and summarize informal and formal discussions via the Internet or e-mail. They can share what they have learned with other candidates at support sessions.

Getting Started

- Facilitators can assist the potential candidate in determining whether there is a good match between him or her and the certificate field he or she is attempting.

- As early as possible, facilitators should establish a support group consisting of the candidates, facilitators, and other resource people who can help the candidates with specific parts of their portfolios. The resource people might include content specialists, NBCTs, and others (see Chapter 2 for other ideas).

- Once a support group is established, the facilitator should set up a regular (preferably weekly) schedule for meetings. The meetings must allow enough time to review portfolio entries, review assessments, discuss accomplishments, and answer questions about various portfolio activities.

- Although facilitators should become familiar with the NBPTS materials for all certificates, they should focus more on the certificates in which they will be most closely working with candidates.

- The facilitator should encourage each candidate to chart an individual timeline that will merge the instructional program and the portfolio entries.

- The facilitator should help candidates break the process into manageable pieces and then complete each component in a timely fashion so that they will be successful.

- The candidate should commit to the project early and be fully aware of the amount of work required to complete the entire assessment process.

- Early in the process candidates must read all the relevant materials provided by the

NBPTS. Candidates will then be able to indicate to the facilitator which areas are problematic for them and will require special help.

- The facilitator should encourage the candidate to begin collecting documented accomplishments for the professional portfolio early in the process.

- In the classroom, candidates should explain the purpose of their portfolio activities to their students before they begin work on it. Students can help teachers to make quality videotapes and written work.

- The facilitator can assist candidates by enlisting the support of their schools' administrators. Make sure the principal understands the purpose of NBPTS certification and is willing to provide the needed support (audio-visual, copying, noise control, etc.).

- Facilitators should encourage candidates to network with other teachers and experts in their own areas, consider joining organizations related to their areas, and attend professional conferences.

Standards

- Facilitators should encourage candidates to familiarize themselves with the standards, discuss the standards with colleagues, and reflect on and document how the standards are being met in their classrooms.

- Facilitators should encourage candidates who have completed an entry to highlight each standard with a different color marker to show how each one is addressed in the entry. This activity will confirm for the candidates that what they do already reflects the standards.

Portfolio

- Facilitators should urge each candidate to set up a place at home (and/or at school) for his or her files, and encourage the candidate to update the files daily.

- The facilitator and the candidate should jointly review the portfolio materials sent to each candidate.

- The facilitator should make sure that each candidate thoroughly reads all directions for all entries of the portfolio in their chosen field of certification. The facilitator should advise the candidate to make connections between the entries and his or her own curriculum. The candidate should determine which lessons best suit the portfolio entries.

- The facilitator should direct the candidate's attention to the section entitled "How Will My Response Be Scored?" in each portfolio. Make sure candidates compare their early drafts to the listed criteria for success. It is helpful to have the facilitator or a colleague make the comparisons with the candidate; another perspective often reveals unintended omissions, and also confirms successful demonstration of the standards.

- The facilitator should have the candidate reread all the analysis prompts for each type of activity before planning the activity. This will provide the necessary structure for responding to the prompts in each analysis.

- The facilitator should help the candidate build an individual timeline that will merge the instructional program and the portfolio tasks. Plan the portfolio in chunks so that the candidate gathers general information for a while and then focuses on one entry and carries it to completion before beginning another when possible.

- After the timeline is complete, the facilitator should encourage the candidate to stick to it.

- The facilitator should encourage the candidate to share collected examples with others. Facilitators should urge the candidate to plan a lesson or unit in collaboration with another teacher, or even to go observe another teacher teach a similar lesson.

- The facilitator *must* remind the candidates that the NBPTS requires a signed release form for each student whose work is analyzed or who appears on a videotape. Advise the candidates to give theses forms to students as soon as possible. If parents deny permission, their children cannot be included in videotaped scenes nor can their written exercises be included for evaluation.

- The facilitator can suggest that candidates make use of Parents' Night or a similar activity to inform parents of the taping and assignment-collection activities that will take place during the year. When the candidate meets with parents, he or she should explain why he or she may need their assistance for the Documented Accomplishments portion of the portfolio. Parents will be more likely to cooperate if they know exactly what the purpose of the activity is to be.

- Some entry components require collecting materials over time and then analyzing them. Facilitators should advise candidates to start their collections early but wait to analyze them until they are ready to focus on that entry.

- Facilitators should remind candidates to organize their responses in the order indicated in the directions. This ensures that NBPTS assessors can find evidence when they score the response, since they do not know the candidate's students.

- Facilitators should encourage candidates to develop their analysis skills over time by periodically taping and analyzing classroom work. In all entries candidates are expected to describe, analyze, and reflect on the lessons they present.

- Facilitators should advise candidates to break down their lessons into observable tasks, answering questions such as: Which standards are exhibited? What obvious problems stand out? Are there surprises? How would this lesson be changed to benefit students?

- Facilitators should meet with the candidates regularly and perhaps more frequently as the deadlines near. Begin with the standards, then address the process of analysis.

Videotaping: Technical Aspects

- At the outset, facilitators need to read all the materials on videotaping that are included in the portfolio and then encourage candidates to do the same.

- Facilitators must encourage candidates to start videotaping early. Advise candidates to videotape often; to videotape all classes; to experiment to find the best places in their classrooms for the students and their desks, the camera, the camera operator, and themselves;

to pay close attention to the lighting (natural and artificial); and to experiment with recording sound (wearing a body microphone is very helpful).

- Facilitators should warn candidates to consider the first two or three videotapes as practice ones. The students need to overcome the "Hi, mom!" phenomenon, and the candidate needs to become comfortable with seeing him- or herself on video.

- The facilitator should advise the candidate to confer with the camera person. If a candidate works regularly with the same camera person, he or she can establish signals to use during a taping to cue the camera person either to focus on the teacher or to focus on a student or group of students.

- Facilitators should remind candidates that they must comment on the interactions of the students in the class to demonstrate their knowledge of the unique capabilities of each learner.

- Facilitators should arrange for candidates to review one video before they make the next one so that they learn from their mistakes. If possible, they should review videos made by other teachers from their school or from their support group for critiquing.

Videotaping: Analysis

- Candidates should always plan to do about three times as many lessons, tapes, student collections, and so on as required so they will have ample choices when they are ready to compile final drafts.

- Facilitators should encourage candidates to videotape and analyze multiple lessons, starting early in the year.

- The candidate should choose topics that will engage and hold the interest of the class. The candidate should plan various activities during the taping time.

- Facilitators can assist in the analysis of videotapes by pointing out alternative approaches to the lesson and explaining why such approaches should or should not be used. The candidate should work through these steps alone. Then he or she should share the tape and the analysis with a trusted colleague or with the facilitator and look for points of agreement or disagreement.

- The facilitator should advise the candidate to tell the video operator to focus on student faces as they speak—the impact of the lesson will show up on their faces.

- On all videotaped entries, candidates should practice description, analysis, and reflection.

Reflective Practice

- Teachers don't have much extra time. Facilitators should advise candidates to incorporate reflection and analysis time into their daily routines early because this time will prove invaluable later.

- Facilitators should encourage candidates to reflect on their work. The NBPTS is not looking for perfection in a teacher: it is seeking candidates who have the ability to grow, to change, and to continually improve. Candidates should be encouraged to write about their own change over time.

- Facilitators should consistently make the point that recording observations and describing what happened is not analysis. Candidates need to discuss the impact of their actions on student learning and to reflect on what went well, what needs to be changed, and why.

- Facilitators should encourage candidates to develop their analytical skills over time by periodically taping and analyzing themselves. Keeping reflective journals in which they record what worked, what didn't work, ideas for change, and reasons to attempt changes is another way to increase the effectiveness of self-analysis.

- Facilitators should help teachers develop their reflective skills by suggesting they ask themselves questions, such as:

  Each day do I reflect on my practice (before, after, and even in the middle of a lesson)?
  How am I meeting my students needs?
  How can I best further my students' in their learning?
  What else do I need to know?
  Is there a resource I need to make my lesson better?
  Do I exist within a total community of learners and invite students, parents, colleagues, and community leaders to be a part of our daily environment?
  How do I share what I learn with others?

- Facilitators should encourage candidates to look at why things worked or didn't work. Candidates shouldn't be afraid to point out things that surprised them or that turned out differently than expected.

- Facilitators should encourage candidates to ponder questions such as: If I had a chance to teach this lesson over again, how would I change it in the light of the student's response? How would I follow it up? What advice would I give the student?

- The facilitator can guide the candidates in a process of reflection that will lead him or her to better practice. (Sources of information related to reflective practice are included in the Resources list at the end of Chapter 2.)

Written Commentary

- Facilitators should give frequent and honest feedback. If something is not clear to you, it probably won't be clear to the assessors.

- The facilitator should provide the candidate with feedback on the clarity of his or her analysis and the quality of his or her evidence provided in the written commentary.

- Remind candidates that they must provide evidence of the effects of their teaching on student achievement in their written commentaries.

- Facilitators should encourage candidates to be clear in their written commentaries about what belongs where and how things fit together. For example, they should use clear headings and bold type where appropriate.

- Facilitators should urge candidates to use outlines to organize written commentary.

- Candidates should read all directions thoroughly and think about entry requirements before writing.

- Be sure candidates strictly adhere to page and type size limitations.

Developing a Student Case Study

Facilitators should encourage candidates to consider the following when an entry requires a student case study (e.g., a child's literacy development).

- Plan how long the study will last, based on the criteria of the study and your initial reading and writing assessment of the student. Develop a timeline for the study.

- Plan ahead by penciling in the times you will be working with the student in your lesson plan book. In this way they will become routine.

- Send home a questionnaire asking parents for specific information on background and literacy behaviors observed in the home. (See Chapter 4 and Appendix 4.1.)

- Meet with the student's parents to share testing results, explain your plans for the student for the approximate eight-week period, receive your signed permission slip, and share ideas with the parents concerning how they can help their child at home.

- Place the student release form in your file.

- Think of relevant, meaningful activities to improve your home–school partnership with the family of the child in your study.

- Develop a way to organize the information about the child. For instance, keep all notes and assessment data about the student in one folder or on one clipboard. Be sure to date all documentation.

- Select many samples of the student's work. Lay them on a large surface. Review the portfolio criteria, relevant standards, and questions.

- While always keeping the assessment criteria in mind, select the samples you will use for your portfolio entry.

- After you develop your entry, turn the information listed under "How Will My Response Be Scored?" into questions for yourself to sure you have all the materials and background on which you will be assessed.

- Always support your findings by stating clear evidence. It is very important not to assume that your assessors will know what you mean. Make a claim and then describe how it is supported by evidence and examples clearly stated in your entry.

Finishing the Portfolio

- Before the final submission, the facilitator should read candidates' entries to comment on them and to ask questions. The facilitator should focus on their connection to all of the prompts and how they provide evidence of the standards.

- The candidates need to be warned that the process of preparing the documents and videotapes for submission is time-consuming and often frustrating. Facilitators may want to suggest the following:

Practice duplicating and copying videotapes. Only the specified number of minutes on each tape will be examined and this means careful copying.

Practice with your particular computer and printer.

Practice fitting your comments into the required forms, especially in the Documented Accomplishments section.

If you cannot make the printer achieve the format, you will have to cut and paste in order to fill the boxes.

Make copies of everything: forms, tapes, the whole works.

Copy as you go! Allow two days for assembling the completed portfolio submission!

Assessment Center

- Have candidate practice by using the samples in the materials sent by the NBPTS.

- If candidates have not taught the subjects covered—for example, statistics, calculus, or discrete math—or the age group—for example, pre-school, kindergarten, or first grade—a good review of the objectives for each area and grade level is definitely needed. Textbooks, a curriculum guide, or any refresher courses provided by your school system or local university would be helpful.

- Most of the questions will test the candidate's knowledge on current thinking in that particular area of education. Thus candidates should be familiar with the standards documents for their content(s).

- Facilitators should note that this is not a standard content test. Pedagogy—how you introduce or illustrate a topic—is a big part of the assessment.

- Encourage candidates to bring all the supplies they are allowed to bring.

- Structuring practice sessions with prompts before candidates attend the assessment center is essential.

Early Childhood/ Generalist

NANCY AREGLADO
MARLENE HENRIQUES
LISA HOLM

Chapter 4 provides facilitators with:

- An overview of the EC/G portfolio entries.
- Assistance in planning activities for support sessions.
- Information about assessment center activities.
- A list of related resources.

CERTIFICATION CHARACTERISTICS

The Early Childhood/Generalist (EC/G) certificate field is designed to document the accomplishments of those who teach children ages three to eight years. This chapter details each portfolio entry for EC/G, highlights the standards as the focus for the required written commentary, and gives examples of sample activities. It also includes hints and activities to assist facilitators in learning about each entry and familiarizing themselves with the NBPTS standards for the EC/G. A Resources list of recommended professional resources is provided at the end of the chapter. The information and recommended activities can be expanded for use with other similar certification fields (e.g., Middle Childhood/Generalist).

The three teacher candidates whose work is presented in this chapter are representative of the uniqueness and wide range of abilities of candidates seeking EC/G certification. Such diversity in roles and teaching situations can assist facilitators as they support teacher candidates.

STANDARDS

Candidates must meet eight standards in their work to achieve NBPTS certification as an EC/G. These standards provide the frame within which EC/G candidates develop their portfolios and prepare for the assessment center activities (NBPTS, EA/G, 1995).

Standard I: Understanding Young Children

Teachers know how young children develop and learn. Their knowledge grows as they observe and learn from their students. Teachers stay current in their knowledge of early childhood development. Teachers use diversity and commonalties in their students as opportunities for learning. They build connections between what they teach and their students' prior knowledge and cultural background.

Standard II: Promoting Child Development and Learning

Teachers promote children's physical, emotional, linguistic, creative, intellectual, social, and cognitive development by organizing the environment in ways that best facilitate the development and learning of young children. They understand the importance of play in children's development. They foster physical health, social skills, emotional development, language acquisition, and positive approaches toward learning.

Standard III: Knowledge of Integrated Curriculum

Based on their knowledge of academic subjects and how young children learn, teachers design and implement child-centered learning experiences within and across the disciplines, including the arts, literacy and English language arts, mathematics, science, and social studies.

Standard IV: Multiple Teaching Strategies for Meaningful Learning

Teachers use a variety of methods and materials to promote individual development, learning, and social cooperation. They use these strategies to help children create their own understanding and learning. They use tasks and materials that accommodate a wide range of abilities; they help children take responsibility for making appropriate choices; and they support and seek help for children with exceptional needs.

Standard V: Assessment

Teachers know the strengths and weaknesses of various assessment methodologies, continually monitor children's activities and behavior, and analyze this information to improve their work with children and parents. Teachers use a mix of assessment instruments, a variety of settings, several forms of reference for assessment, and they assess over a period of time. They use assessment to drive their instruction.

Standard VI: Reflective Practice

Teachers regularly analyze, evaluate, and strengthen the quality and effectiveness of their work. They reflect on each lesson, considering what was effective and what was ineffective in promoting

	Portfolio entry	Standard	Hints	Sample activities	Resources
1	Reflecting on a Teaching and Learning Sequence	Refer to Standards I–V	—Know, discuss, reflect, and document these standards. —Think about your philosophy of early childhood education and development and document this in your work.	—Goals are presented for teaching and learning. —Relation of goals to standards is discussed.	
2	Examining a Child's Literacy Development	Refer to Standards I, III, IV, V, & VII	—Provide clear evidence and examples of child's growth. —Document and state clearly your findings about the child's progress.	—Case study of one child. —Gather information. —Do activities to assess literacy development. —Identify instructional strategies.	*Reading Recovery* (Clay, 1993) Appendix: Parent questionnaire
3	Introduction to Your Classroom Community	Refer to Standards I, II, & IV	—When developing written commentary, ask yourself, "Why did I use or do the activity?"	—Integrate standards into practice. —Reflect on videotapes. —Sample responses documenting: class content; space and materials; rules and routines.	Resources
4	Engaging Children in Science Learning —10-minute videotape —Written commentary	Refer to Standards I–IV	—Develop goals and activities that promote developing hypotheses, test ideas, review findings, and reflection. —Promote student questions. —Model problem solving.	—Instructional context. —Video analysis.	Resources
5 6	Document Accomplishments I, Professional Community Document Accomplishments II, Outreach to Families	I. Refer to Standards II, VIII II. Refer to Standards I, V, VII	—Review standards. —Gather documentation of accomplishments.	—Guiding questions. —Meeting criteria. —Communicating with families and communities.	

Assessment center	Description	Standards	Hints	Sample activities	Resources
	Provide written documentation of your knowledge across the age range three to eight.	Review all standards	—Observe children play in your classroom. —Understand development across the age continuum. —Familiarize yourself with curriculum across the age continuum.	—Play situation. —Math assessment. —Analyzing children's work. —Developing curriculum.	—NBPTS assessment center materials. —Suggested books: see Resources. —Review Entry 2.

FIGURE 4.1. Certification Field Organizer: Early Childhood/Generalist (EC/G).

CERTIFICATION FIELD ORGANIZER

FIELD: _____

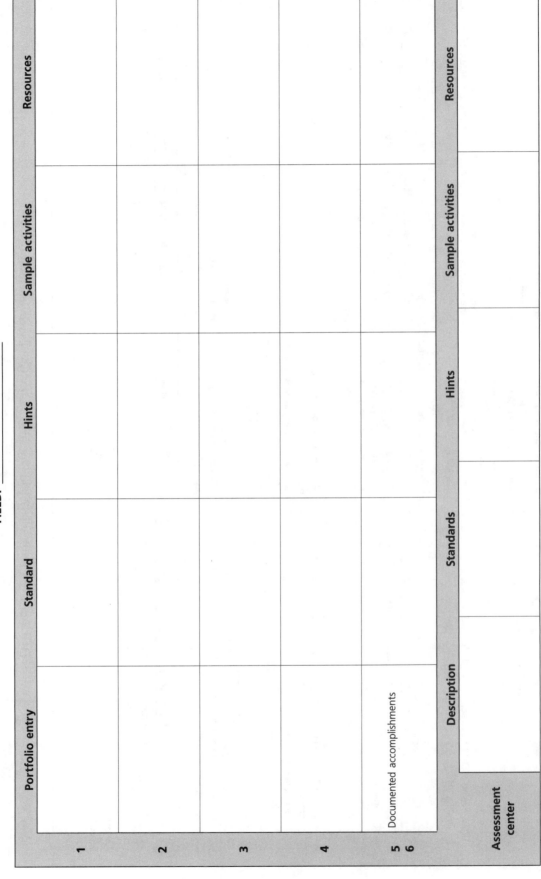

	Portfolio entry	Standard	Hints	Sample activities	Resources
1					
2					
3					
4					
5	Documented accomplishments				
6					

	Description	Standards	Hints	Sample activities	Resources
Assessment center					

FIGURE 4.2. Blank field organizer. From *Preparing Teachers for National Board Certification* by Kathleen Anderson Steeves and Barbara Cole Browne. Copyright 2000 by The Guilford Press. Permission to reproduce this figure is granted to purchasers of this book for personal use only (see copyright page for details).

72

student learning. Teachers ask colleagues for insight, are open to new ideas, and continually learn from prevailing research.

Standard VII: Family Partnerships

Teachers work with and through parents and families to support children's learning and development. They provide information to parents about their program and ways parents can extend classroom learning activities. They work with parents in planning school programs and in finding support services for their children. Teachers work effectively with parent volunteers and encourage parent participation in classroom activities.

Standard VIII: Professional Partnerships

Teachers work with colleagues, parents, and a variety of other people in the community to improve programs and practices for young children and their families. Teachers impart their knowledge to their colleagues and take an active role in the formulation of policies affecting children. Through workshops, research, projects, and presentations, they contribute to the advancement of early childhood education.

HINTS FOR FACILITATORS

✔ As EC/G candidates begin planning how to develop their portfolio entries, facilitators should stress the importance of taking note of which standards are required for specific portfolio entries. The standards need to be integrated throughout the process of setting goals and implementing curriculum, developing learning activities, assessing students' learning, developing lesson plans, and engaging in self-reflection and self-assessment.

✔ Facilitators should help candidates to familiarize themselves with the standards for each entry.

✔ Facilitators must keep in mind that interpretation of the standards is based on each teacher candidate's perception of and philosophy regarding early childhood education. Facilitators and candidates will benefit from discussing the standards in relation to the teacher's individual philosophy within a small group of EC/G candidates.

✔ Facilitators should network with early childhood teachers and experts in the early childhood field.

✔ Facilitators should encourage candidates to join early childhood organizations such as the National Association for the Education of Young Children (NAEYC).

CERTIFICATION FIELD ORGANIZER

The Certification Field Organizer (Figure 4.1) can be used to plan individual entry discussions and to help structure your work with EC/G candidates. We also provide a blank organizer (Figure 4.2), in which facilitators can add ideas as they guide candidates through the development of the portfolio and preparation for the assessment center activities.

The Certification Field Organizer contains a summary of the entries, standards, and activities that are detailed in the remainder of this chapter.

CREATING EARLY CHILDHOOD/GENERALIST PORTFOLIO ENTRIES

The following sections provide a description of the activities and learning experiences designed to address each of the six required portfolio entries, as summarized in the Certification Field Organizer. We provide the facilitator with specific information regarding the EG/C portfolio development and assessment center activities.

Entry 1: Reflecting on a Teaching and Learning Sequence

Description

This portfolio entry focuses on students' work. It requires the candidate to describe a sequence of activities involving extended exploration of a theme or topic that draws on concepts from social studies and the arts and builds strong ties with children's families. Candidates are required to prepare a written commentary on their teaching practices and explain how these practices meet the particular standard being addressed. Supporting documentation is required to demonstrate instructional approaches related to learning experiences and assessment methods and products.

In planning for this entry, the candidate must develop three goals that state what children will learn and the skills they will develop. The candidate's familiarity with and understanding of EC/G Standards I–VII is critical, as they provide the framework that an accomplished teacher uses.

Standards to Be Addressed

The specific standards addressed in this entry are:

Standard I: Understanding Young Children
Standard II: Promoting Child Development and Learning
Standard III: Knowledge of Integrated Curriculum
Standard IV: Multiple Teaching Strategies for Meaningful Learning
Standard V: Assessment
Standard VI: Reflective Practice
Standard VII: Family Partnerships

Hint for Facilitators

✔ Sharing practice and strategies across the age range is essential in developing clear responses to this entry.

Activities for Assisting Candidates

In planning how to develop goals and activities for "Reflecting on a Teaching and Learning Sequence," each teacher's philosophy should guide the development of the goals and must link to the standards. For example, a teacher may believe that children construct knowledge through active exploration and interaction with people and materials. In this case, the teacher will reflect that belief in the classroom by providing opportunities for "hands-on, minds-on" experiences by using various peer groupings that meet the needs of all learners (Standard I: Understanding Young Children, and Standard IV: Multiple Teaching Strategies for Meaningful Learning). As each candidate moves through the certification process, he or she will further elucidate his or her philosophy and provide evidence of how that philosophy relates to the standards.

ACTIVITY 1: DEVELOPING GOALS AND RELATING TO STANDARDS

Facilitators should have each candidate select a topic/theme he or she covers in the classroom, develop a goal and related objectives for the theme, and discuss how the EC/G standards relate to that goal and those objectives. A sample of a teachers' response is described below and can be used by facilitators to guide discussion.

Sample Response. Using the topic of families as a theme, a kindergarten teacher developed a goal stating that students will identify self as a unique person in the family. Specific objectives for this goal included developing children's understanding that (1) the composition of a family differs; (2) a child may be the only child or have many brothers and sisters, be the firstborn or the last born, and so on; and (3) families are alike in some ways and different in others.

The sample activity relates to the standards in the following manner. The teacher interwove activities incorporating Standards I, II, III, IV, V, VI, and VII in developing this entry. The children drew pictures of the members of their families using a variety of materials: crayons, paints, markers, or the computer (Standard IV). Each child created his or her drawing and/or writing at his or her own level (Standard I). The children used the home living center to role-play family members in various situations (Standard II). The children read stories about human families (*Peter's Chair*) and animal families (an informational book on how dolphins take care of their young); graphed the number of people in each family; sorted plastic bears according to size and color; and used puppets of family members to act out stories (Standard III). The teacher assessed the children's work in terms of their drawing and writing progress, their concept of ordinal numbers, and their classification and sorting skills (Standard V). The students created a class book with drawings and stories about each child's family, and then took the book home and shared with families. Parents were invited in to class to share cultural traditions with the class (Standard VII).

ACTIVITY 2: PROMOTING SELF-REFLECTION

The goals developed by the teacher should guide all aspects of planning for the specified theme. Careful attention to the EC/G standards enables the teacher to develop a valid overall plan with related experiences that demonstrate a sequential flow and build upon one another. Reflective thinking becomes a critical element during implementation of these experiences.

Use the sample response provided for Activity 1 or have candidates bring in their own. Have the candidates discuss lessons with their colleagues in small groups. This provides the candidates with further insight and knowledge and helps them make informed decisions that strengthen the quality of their teaching and make linkages to the NBPTS standards. Self-reflection is crucial in demonstrating the level of an individual teacher's practice and is an important part of the portfolio process.

Examining class activities provides the teacher with valuable information. If an activity goes well, the teacher analyzes what made it successful and thinks about how that success can be duplicated in other situations. If the activity does not go well, the teacher analyzes problem areas and reflects on how to revise and change instruction in the future. As the teacher interacts with the students and assesses both the process the students used and their work products, he or she gains information that allows him or her to make adaptations and modifications to meet the needs of the learners.

Entry 2: Examining a Child's Literacy Development

Description

This entry requires a written commentary and supporting artifacts that will show how well a teacher can assess and support children's literacy development. The particular focus of this entry is on one child's literacy development and how the teacher's literacy strategies and activities supported and enhanced the child's learning.

Standards to be Addressed

The specific standards to be addressed in this entry are:

> Standard I: Understanding Young Children
> Standard III: Knowledge of Integrated Curriculum
> Standard IV: Multiple Teaching Strategies for Meaningful Learning
> Standard V: Assessment
> Standard VII: Family Partnerships

Hints for Facilitators

✔ Encourage candidates to review and discuss Standards I, III, IV, V, and VII and compare them with the requirements for this entry *before* they plan any actual lessons.

✔ Encourage candidates to review their authentic assessment class records and to select the students who could profit the most from this type of intensive literacy instruction.

✔ Have candidates select three or four children whose reading and writing they would like to study intensively for at least eight weeks. For the final portfolio, the candidate will present one child's literacy development as a case example; by monitoring three or four children, the candidate will be able to select the best case.

✔ Encourage candidates to test students to determine their baseline abilities and determine the appropriate next steps for each child.

✔ Candidates should consider the following questions about each student: Where is each child in his or her literacy development? What are the needs of each child? What is the child's stage of development in the reading and writing process?

✔ Gather as much information about the child as possible. Include parents in the information-gathering process by sending home a parent questionnaire (see Appendix 4.1 for a sample) and then incorporate this data into your background information on the child.

Activities for Assisting Candidates

This entry requires the candidate to (1) assess a child's literacy development (see Activities 1 and 2), (2) design appropriate instructional strategies (see Activity 5), and (3) demonstrate the child's literacy development (see Activities 3 and 4).

ACTIVITY 1: ASSESSING LITERACY DEVELOPMENT

Have the candidates brainstorm as a group to decide which types of formal and informal assessments they will use to develop a baseline in writing, reading, and language levels at the beginning of the study. Assign candidates the task of beginning to assess a child in their class and sharing the information at the next support session. Remind the candidates to record the date of each assessment piece (these will become artifacts).

Sample Response. A reading specialist used the Individual Writing Checklist in *Let's Write* (Dill & Areglado, 1997) to assess writing development throughout the study. In addition, the specialist noted the percentage of words in invented spelling (spelling that resembles the sounds students hear) versus standard spelling, whether the message was meaningful, and whether the spacing was ample.

The specialist taught the student how to stretch out the sounds in words, so that both the initial and final sounds are distinctly sounded out and heard. The specialist developed a word bank of high-frequency "known words," words the child can either read or write. As another activity, the specialist placed the student in a literacy group with several other students who had similar needs. She taught reading strategies to a parent volunteer to provide one-on-one help to the child. This variety of activities demonstrated the use of multiple teaching strategies for positive learning.

When the reading specialist compared early test results of the student's literacy level to test results two and one-half months later, she noted a 17% increase of the words in the sample in standard spelling.

ACTIVITY 2: ASSESSING LITERACY DEVELOPMENT USING MULTIPLE STRATEGIES

Multiple strategies deserve consideration when assessing a child's literacy development. Encourage candidates to practice assessing and monitoring a child's literacy development in various ways, for example, with anecdotal records, running records (Clay, 1993; Fountas & Pinnell, 1997), and observations. A sample of anecdotal records is given in Appendix 4.2.

ACTIVITY 3: DEMONSTRATING A CHILD'S LITERACY DEVELOPMENT— IDENTIFYING STRENGTHS AND NEEDS

Assign the candidates the task of using one child's development as an example to share in the support session. Suggest that the candidate look at all three areas of student literacy growth— reading, writing, and speaking—and compare the child's literacy progress in each of the three areas. Evidence may surface about areas where the child's progress is hampered. One goal for the candidate would be to help the child advance in those problem areas. By sharing a number of examples, candidates will broaden their understanding of children's literacy development.

Sample Response. A first-grade teacher assessed a student's reading skills by checking the student's knowledge of concepts about print, asking him to recite the alphabet, dictating words for him to write, having him read and write high-frequency first-grade words, and administering running record tests of the student's reading. The teacher noted that the child progressed more quickly in writing than in reading. The teacher was then able to build on the child's writing skills and identify strategies to strengthen the child's reading skills.

ACTIVITY 4: DEMONSTRATING LITERACY DEVELOPMENT—GATHERING EVIDENCE

Facilitators should encourage candidates to gather general information and specific hard data about the child's literacy development in several areas, including print awareness, drawing and writing, assessing oral language, and story retelling. A sample (see Appendix 4.2) can be used to assess and demonstrate a child's literacy development. The candidates can share their experiences and artifacts at support sessions.

ACTIVITY 5: DESIGNING APPROPRIATE INSTRUCTIONAL STRATEGIES—
DESCRIBING AND ANALYZING

This next activity provides facilitators with evidence regarding how candidates identify appropriate instructional strategies. Ask the candidates to analyze each literacy product and then choose those pieces that illustrate the next step in the child's development to bring to the support session. During the session individual candidates should discuss the salient evidence of progress in each artifact that he or she includes in his or her entries. Such discussion might include the observations the teacher made in watching the child perform the task.

Sample Response. The following excerpt describes how a candidate might describe and analyze a child's literacy development.

> "The student was tentative in her writing at first. She held her pencil and crayons apprehensively. Artifact 1 shows large, poorly formed letters. Later the student began to hold her writing tools more confidently. Artifact 2 demonstrates her use of stronger lines and smaller letters, indicating that her small motor control has increased and that she is more sure of her writing."

Candidates should provide clear convincing evidence that demonstrates how to individualize the child's program to move him or her to the next level. For example:

> "In analyzing Artifact 4, I see that John has a good understanding of beginning and ending sounds. He used an 'l' and a 'k' to write the word 'like.' In each of his words he has a close approximation to the actual first and last letter sound. My goal in the next few weeks will be for John to hear more middle sounds in words. I will do this by stretching out the sounds more when I meet with him, by asking him to listen for middle sounds, and by pointing out the middle sounds in words as I read aloud to the class."

Entry 3: Introduction to Your Classroom Community

Description

This entry provides the teacher with the opportunity to describe in detail the physical environment in which he or she teaches and explain how this environment supports the emotional and social development of the students. The teacher describes his or her philosophy and goals and shows how rules and routines support this philosophy.

This entry requires the teacher to develop a written commentary that describes how the teacher encourages and builds children's emotional and social skills, with an emphasis on creating and sustaining a climate that supports an appreciation of diversity. The commentary must be supported and illustrated by an unedited 10-minute videotape of classroom interactions.

There are two components of this entry: the written commentary and the videotape. The written commentary must meet two goals: (1) to demonstrate how children show respect, resolve conflicts, and develop their social skills; and (2) to discuss diversity within the classroom and the community and describe ways in which this diversity is appreciated. These goals must be addressed in terms of three different elements:

1. The teaching setting and the characteristics of the children
2. The way space and materials are used to enhance learning
3. The rules and routines the teacher uses to meet the two goals.

The second part of this entry calls for a videotape of the community of learners. This unedited tape must show the teacher interacting with at least eight children and engaging in a meaningful event that relates to the above-stated goals. This videotape actually shows the classroom described in the written part of this entry, includes no text, and illustrates the practice of the rules and routines discussed earlier. Reflection about the videotape must address the event, the significance of the event, and an evaluation of the video.

Standards to Be Addressed

This entry is evaluated with emphasis on three standards:

Standard I. Understanding Young Children
Standard II: Promoting Child Development and Learning
Standard IV: Multiple Teaching Strategies for Meaningful Learning

Hints for Facilitators

✔ Encourage candidates to outline this entry. The outline can be used both as a guide for support group discussion and to organize the written commentary.

✔ Engage candidates in discussions around topics such as expectations concerning student behavior, values they promote in the classroom, and strategies they teach for conflict resolution.

Activities for Assisting Candidates

ACTIVITY 1: DISCUSSING AND ORGANIZING RESPONSES

Facilitators can guide candidates toward documenting their teaching in the three components for this entry by using the questions below to promote discussion.

In what ways do I promote child development and learning (Standard II) in the classroom?
How is learning organized (e.g., centers) so that the children have easy access to the materials?
How do I make decisions about the curriculum?
How do I provide for the learning of *all* children?
How does learning take place when altercations occur?
What techniques are used to ensure that learning occurs for *all* children?

For further discussion, facilitators could use the following questions to help teachers think about their classrooms:

- What underlying values do you use to develop the classroom community?
- How do you establish rules and routines with your students?
- How do you create a caring classroom in which each child recognizes him- or herself as a valued, unique, and contributing member?
- How do you help students develop concepts such as respect for others?
- What principles guide you in setting up the physical classroom environment?

Additional activities to help facilitators guide candidates can be found in Appendix 4.3. They relate to the teaching setting and the characteristics of children (Activity 2); use of space and materials (Activity 3); rules and routines (Activity 4); and reflecting on the videotape (Activity 5).

Entry 4: Engaging Children in Science Learning

Description

This portfolio entry requires the teacher to discuss and analyze a featured learning experience, explaining how it fits into an instructional sequence and how it reflects the teacher's general approach to science instruction. Candidates are required to prepare a written commentary and a videotape that illustrates the teacher's skills in facilitating students' acquisition of scientific knowledge.

The written commentary and the videotape prepared for this entry must feature a learning experience that is one of a series of three or more related science-learning experiences. These experiences must be designed to heighten children's awareness and understanding of science concepts and to increase their utilization of scientific skills, such as observing, thinking, and communicating.

Standards to Be Addressed

Six standards apply to this entry:

Standard I: Understanding Young Children
Standard II: Promoting Child Development and Learning
Standard III: Knowledge of Integrated Curriculum
Standard IV: Multiple Teaching Strategies for Meaningful Learning
Standard V: Assessment
Standard VII: Reflective Practice

Hints for Facilitators

✔ Encourage candidates to explore the "Big Ideas," the overarching concepts, during science instruction.

✔ Engage in collegial conversations regarding the overarching concepts in science instruction.

✔ Encourage candidates to become knowledgeable about resources such as Gardner's *Frames of Mind: The Theory of Multiple Intelligences* (1993). (See Resources at the end of this chapter for other suggested readings.)

✔ Consider the role that student inquiry plays in the instructional process.

✔ Begin to plan your series of science learning experiences based on what students *need* to know versus what students *want* to know.

✔ Incorporate vivid experiences that will enable students to make connections between what they already know and new information. Make science come alive for your students.

✔ Continually ask yourself why you are doing what you are doing and what impact it has on student learning.

✔ Consider ways to involve families in the scientific process both in the classroom and at home.

Activities for Assisting Candidates

ACTIVITY 1: INCORPORATING STANDARDS INTO WRITTEN COMMENTARY

Facilitators could encourage candidates to incorporate the standards throughout their portfolio entries. For example, candidates should draw upon their understanding of child development and their knowledge of their own students to create learning experiences that challenge, provide meaning, and engage interest (Standard I: Understanding Young Children). Knowing that children construct knowledge through interactions with people and materials enables the candidate to design experiences for all children to grow in both knowledge and understanding of science. Other examples of incorporating the standards are listed in Appendix 4.3.

ACTIVITY 2: INSTRUCTIONAL CONTEXT—BRAINSTORMING

The candidate must discuss the concepts she or he wants the children to acquire through a particular exercise, as well as the scientific process the children employ during their explorations. During the support session have candidates brainstorm the scientific concepts they plan to cover and the scientific processes their children will use in the exploration. Such sharing will expand the candidates' ideas regarding teaching science. In determining goals for the science sequence, candidates must consider both the "Big Ideas" in science and the particular needs and interests of their students. This double consideration helps the candidate to clarify why he or she chose specific goals.

Candidates *must* describe how the specific learning experiences discussed in this section of the entry address the overall goals and concepts for the sequence of study.

ACTIVITY 3: VIDEOTAPE ANALYSIS—VIDEO CONTEXT

The Videotape Analysis is divided into four subsections: Video Context, Learning Community, Reflecting on the Videotape, and Evaluating the Learning. Each section is addressed through a written commentary. The following activity explores the Video Context.

Facilitators can encourage candidates to consider questions such as: What are the linked events that immediately precede and/or follow those shown on the tape? What are the specific goals for the featured learning experience? Encourage candidates to bring in their own examples to share and discuss.

ACTIVITY 4: VIDEOTAPE ANALYSIS—THE LEARNING COMMUNITY

The candidate should ask him- or herself How did I stimulate children's thinking and learning during the featured learning experience? The candidate must be able to explain how the particular organization and implementation of the experience accommodated different learning needs of children in the class. Specific examples from the videotape *must* be cited.

ACTIVITY 5: VIDEO ANALYSIS—REFLECTING ON THE VIDEOTAPE

In this section the candidate critically considers such questions as: How could I do the lesson differently if I were to do it again? What evidence is there that the learning resulting from the featured experience impacted subsequent lessons and in what ways? In other words, how did the teacher capitalize on successes and revisit missed opportunities? Candidates could share their videotapes in the support group sessions and reflect on these questions.

ACTIVITY 6: VIDEOTAPE ANALYSIS—EVALUATING THE LEARNING

As candidates view the video they should consider the following questions: To what extent were the learning goals for the entire science sequence met? Was my teaching effective? How do I know? How do the children in the class respond to the lesson? Do the children appear to be learning? Again, remind candidates to refer to specific incidents from the videotape to support their answers.

Entry 5: Documented Accomplishments— Collaboration in the Professional Community

Description

The first section of Documented Accomplishments focuses on the EC/G candidate's contributions to the professional community. What important interactions did the candidate have while working with colleagues, with other school personnel, and with the local community? Candidates should think not only about what they have accomplished, but about what tangible evidence, such as a colleague's verification or some type of document, could be used to support their descriptions. "Hard" evidence must be sent along with the entry as substantiation. The total length of the evidence must not exceed 15 pages. A one-page interpretive summary is required at the end of the entry.

Candidates are asked to classify their documented accomplishments over the last five years in three distinct areas:

1. Accomplishments in contributions to the development or review of instructional resources and/or practices, including curricula, instruction, and assessment.
2. Accomplishments in contributions to educational policy and practices through work in professional organizations, colleges, universities, mentoring other teachers, or in other settings.
3. Accomplishments that demonstrate contributions to collaborative work with colleagues in developing pedagogy as a mentor or a learner.

Standards to Be Addressed

The one standard to be addressed in this entry is:

Standard VIII: Professional Partnerships.

Hints for Facilitators

✔ Candidates will need your assistance in deciding what constitutes "accomplishments" and your advice about how to document these accomplishments.

✔ Advise candidates to request verification documents early.

✔ Make sure the candidate understands that the quality of his or her accomplishments is more important than the quantity.

✔ Urge the candidate as he or she reviews his or her professional interactions to look for common threads. These commonalties are useful in helping the candidate determine which accomplishments to highlight as he or she demonstrates the characteristics of a lifelong learner actively sharing with and participating in a community of learners.

Activities for Assisting Candidates

ACTIVITY 1: GUIDING QUESTIONS

Facilitators should have candidates read the criteria for this entry in the portfolio directions. Then encourage the candidates to take information from the standards and develop questions that will help them to decide what to write for the entry. Questions might include:

- How can I show my skill in working with colleagues?
- What have I done in terms of training adults?

  What forum for talking with colleagues have I developed that strengthened my early childhood program?

  What successes have I had with colleagues, administrators, and/or parents?

  What teams have I been involved with that were successful?

  What insights about the early childhood classroom have I given to colleagues and others?

- How have I contributed to the professional development of colleagues and support staff?

  What team am I on where I am responsible for training, managing, and monitoring less-experienced staff members?

  How have I communicated my knowledge of child development and teaching principles to aides, assistants, and volunteers?

  How have I promoted the development of other staff members?

- How have I participated in shaping policies that have affected my students?

  How have I worked to educate policymakers, parents, and citizens about the underlying principles of excellence in early childhood education?

  How have I helped policymakers, parents, and citizens understand how these principles might best be translated into programmatic initiatives?

  Have I informed policymakers, parents, and citizens about relevant early childhood meetings and conferences?

  How have I been effective in decision making regarding early childhood practices?

  How have I voiced my concerns about inappropriate mandates to safeguard the interests of children?

- How have I contributed to the field of early childhood education?

  Have I given workshops, networked, and/or participated in professional organizations or writing that advanced understanding of early childhood education?

  Have I participated in action research and/or collaborative projects or given presentations that shared ideas with colleagues?

Additionally, candidates should refer to their own file of professional accomplishments for the past five years. Candidates might also ask to review administrative files of their accomplishments.

Sometimes teachers forget their noteworthy activities. It is important for facilitators to encourage candidates to take the questions under "Hints" and share them with their administrators and colleagues. Ask them to reflect on each question and then to write down what activities they recall the candidate has done.

ACTIVITY 2: MEETING THE CRITERIA

Brainstorm with candidates a list of activities that would fit under the umbrella of each of the three criteria for this entry and share documentation for each criteria.

Entry 6: Documented Accomplishments—Outreach to Families and Community

Description

This section focuses on the candidate's interactions with students' families and the community at large. Outreach to families is a key component of the accomplished early childhood teacher's practice. While many areas of the EC/G standards address involvement with families, Standards I, V, and VII particularly mention outreach to and collaboration with families.

This entry is designed to examine that part of the professional's practice that occurs outside the classroom. It is important to note that this entry is intended to address the *real significance* of the teacher's interactions with families and the community, rather than the volume of these activities.

This section provides many specific examples of accomplished practice in the area of outreach. These examples do not constitute an exhaustive list; they are offered as a guide for the facilitator to share with candidates. Teachers are asked to examine and document as thoroughly as possible their work and contributions outside the classroom, in particular in the school, with student families, and in the local community. Each contribution and activity must be documented; such documentation includes verification by a knowledgeable witness or corroborator.

Candidates are asked to consider their practice and then to classify their work in one or more ways under three distinct areas. Response to the first area is mandatory.

1. Accomplishments within the current year that demonstrate how the candidate has created ongoing interactive communication with families and other adults about students' progress and learning.
2. Accomplishments within the current year that demonstrate the candidate's consistent effort to understand parents' concerns about student learning, subject matter, and curriculum.
3. Accomplishments within the last five years that demonstrate substantial contribution to connecting the school program to community needs, resources, and interests.

In recognition of the interconnectedness of the accomplished teacher's practice, candidates are required to write a brief interpretive summary as a final reflective activity for this entry. This allows the candidate to reflect on the totality of his or her practice and contributions.

Standards to Be Addressed

This entry particularly emphasizes three standards:

> Standard I: Understanding Young Children
> Standard V: Assessment
> Standard VII: Family Partnerships

Hints for Facilitators

✔ Candidates will need your assistance both in citing their contributions and outreach efforts in establishing school, family, and community partnerships and in documenting their accomplishments.

✔ Encourage candidates to brainstorm with colleagues to develop lists of the ways in which fellow teachers encourage and maintain school–home connections. Next, colleagues should brainstorm ideas for evidence, hard or soft, that would support the authenticity of these connections and of their own contributions.

✔ Encourage candidates to brainstorm with colleagues to develop lists of the ways in which they and others have utilized community resources, as well as ways in which they have formed community partnerships that enhance the educational program.

Activities for Assisting Candidates

ACTIVITY 1: FAMILY PARTNERSHIPS

After reading the portfolio directions and criteria for this entry, the candidate should review Standard VII: Family Partnerships. Encourage candidates to take information from the standard and turn it into questions that will help them brainstorm. The following questions may prove useful to candidates:

- How do I communicate effectively with parents and families to inform and enhance support for children's learning?

  What methods have I used to inform parents about their children's learning?
  What insight have I given parents into their children's learning?
  What measures have I taken to ensure that parents have awareness of strategies they can utilize to support their children's learning?
  What have I done to encourage two-way communication?
  What have I done to involve students in these processes?

- How do I work effectively with families and community volunteers in classroom and school activities?

  What do I do to encourage families to participate in classroom and school activities?
  What do I do to involve community members in the daily activities of the classroom?

What do I do to provide training experiences for individuals who volunteer on an ongoing basis?
How do I help families realize that they are an integral part of our community of learners?

- How do I assist families in supporting their children's learning and development at home?

  What information do I communicate about students' growth and development?
  What kinds of training opportunities and resource materials do I provide for families?
  What do I do to encourage families to become involved in their children's learning expe-
    riences?

- How do I work effectively with parents in decision-making roles and on policy issues?

  How do I involve parents in the instructional decision-making process?
  What do I do to help parents stay informed concerning classroom, school, and district
    policies?

- How do I assist families in obtaining support and services to help their children?

  What do I do to monitor children's needs?
  What do I do to inform parents of available support and services?
  What steps do I take to ensure that students receive the necessary support and services?
  What do I do to become aware of students' needs outside the classroom walls?

ACTIVITY 2: CREATING LISTS

Ongoing communication and other forms of outreach are sometimes so embedded in a teacher's
practice that he or she overlooks particular activities as efforts contributing to family and community partnerships. Facilitators should brainstorm with candidates to create a list of activities that
would fit under the umbrella of each of the three criteria for this entry.

   In developing this entry, candidates should consider all the avenues they utilize in promoting a
true partnership approach to students' learning. Family support and involvement enables the student to access the optimal educational experience. Recognizing this, the accomplished teacher
develops strategies and action plans that will most effectively embrace his or her family population.

ASSESSMENT CENTER PREPARATION

Once the candidate completes and submits his or her portfolio entries to the NBPTS, he or she
immediately moves on to preparing for the second component of the assessment process: assessment at the assessment center.

Description

Prior to the testing date, the candidate will receive a packet of "stimulus materials" concerning
the assessment center activities. The packet addresses the content areas that will be assessed,
includes sample prompts (activities that might be included at the center), and describes the format of the assessments.

Currently, candidates must answer four essay questions for the EC/G Certificate. Each question is devoted to a separate content area and addresses children ages three to eight. Ninety minutes are allowed for each essay. There is a short break between essays, as well as a lunch break. Candidates should plan to spend a full day at the assessment center (currently a Sylvan Learning Center).

The packet of information describing the assessment center activities includes information on testing dates and location. The candidate selects the desired date and location, and schedules his or her appointment. In responding to the essay questions, the candidate may use a computer or write in long hand.

Candidates may bring materials (notes, books, resources) into the assessment center: however, all materials brought to the assessment center must be left at the center. These materials will not be returned. The candidate should be sure that he or she takes only materials that he or she is willing to leave. It is also important to be selective in the materials one takes, as the 90-minute time frame does not allow the candidate a great deal of time to refer to resources.

Standards to Be Addressed

All of the standards are addressed in the assessment center activities.

Hints for Facilitators

✔ The candidate must be familiar with all of the EC/G standards in order to respond to the essay questions posed at the assessment center. These standards provide a framework for the candidate's responses.

✔ Encourage candidates to become familiar with the developmental levels of all children (social, emotional, intellectual, and physical) between ages three and eight, regardless of the specific age level they teach.

✔ Encourage candidates to have professional conversations regarding the developmental stages of children with colleagues such as the art specialist, the speech therapist, and the school psychologist.

✔ Encourage candidates to form support/study groups to prepare themselves for the assessment center.

✔ Arrange for candidates to read about the topics of play, assessment, curriculum development, and analyzing children's work, or encourage them to meet with experts in those areas. Remind them to incorporate ideas from their sources in their responses.

✔ Alert candidates that when responding to the essay questions, they should not assume that the assessor will know what they are thinking. To best convey their thoughts, they should outline their answers, be specific, and give logical reasons (with details) to back up their statements. Most of all, they must show that they *know* their material. This is their time to shine, so they should formulate, polish, and substantiate their ideas.

Activities for Assisting Candidates

The following assessment topics, used in previous years, may serve as a device for candidates to practice timed responses. However, the topics change yearly, so facilitators should encourage candidates to use all the information and suggestions provided by the NBPTS. Candidates should always include responses across the age level of the EC/G certificate field. This will help each candidate understand the content and focus of other grade levels. The following activities can help guide the support session discussions.

Activity 1: Children's Play

This activity area requires the candidate to interpret children's play. The candidate is provided with a transcript of a play situation at a nursery school, kindergarten, or daycare center. The candidate reads the transcript and responds to the questions posed based on his or her observations and interpretations of the play situation.

Questions to consider in preparing for this area include:

What is the purpose of play?
In what ways does it benefit children?
How do you justify having play as a center in your classroom?
What do the experts say about the importance of play?
What do you say to parents who complain that "all the children do is play"?

Consider why play is important in the classroom. Watch children at play and take notes on their conversational interactions. Such presentation will enable the candidate to better visualize and interpret the peer relationships described in the transcript.

Activity 2: Mathematics

The candidate may be asked to take a specific concept or theme within a content such as mathematics (e.g., patterns, geometry, and number relationships) and build a curriculum with specific activities for the grade level the candidate presently teaches.

SAMPLE ACTIVITY

In the kindergarten program themes are usually integrated into the whole curriculum, not treated as a specific subject area. A kindergarten teacher might choose patterns as a theme and give the goals and objectives for that unit. This would be an example of integration using patterns. One goal might be that children understand that a pattern has to repeat.

Activities to reinforce this goal would be reading pattern books where the words repeat or singing songs where the lyrics repeat (language arts), observing seasonal changes and repetitions (science), and using materials such as wooden shapes, colors, letters, and other objects to create patterns (math).

This area is the only one in which the candidate may tailor the response to his or her grade level. In the other three assessments the candidate is specifically told what age or grade level to address in formulating his or her response.

Activity 3: Children's Work

A third assessment activity might focus on samples of children's work in a specific content area and their analysis. The candidate receives samples of work from several children who are in the same grade but who operate at different levels of cognitive development. The samples may be written work and/or drawings. In his or her response, the candidate will discuss the level of understanding that each child demonstrates, identify any misconceptions shown by the work samples, and then detail the next steps necessary to further each child's understanding of the concepts being taught.

Activity 4: Instructional Plan

A fourth assessment activity may involve developing an instructional plan to meet the needs of a specific student. The candidate reviews several literacy samples from a specific student and is given background information about this student. The candidate then determines the instructional focus that will allow the student to progress in his or her literacy development. In order to respond successfully, the candidate must know the benchmark literacy skills at each grade level, as well as the sequence of learning for literacy skills. Reviewing activities and resources from the portfolio, Entry 2: Literacy Development, can help prepare for this activity.

Activity 5: Sharing with Colleagues

Set up opportunities for candidates to have colleagues from different grade levels share samples of children's work to facilitate a greater understanding of the developmental stages of children at that grade level.

The assessment center activities are demanding and require the candidate to demonstrate an in-depth understanding of the learning process as it relates to children ages three to eight. For optimal performance, the candidate should enter the assessment center well prepared and well rested.

RESOURCES

Ames, L. B., & Haber, C. C. (1990). *Your eight-year-old: Lively and outgoing*. New York: Delta.

Ames, L. B., & Haber, C. C. (1987). *Your seven-year-old: Life in a minor key*. New York: Delta.

Ames, L. B., & Ilg, F. L. (1979). *Your five-year-old: Sunny and serene*. New York: Delta.

Ames, L. B., & Ilg, F. L. (1976). *Your four-year-old: Wild and wonderful*. New York: Delta.

Ames, L. B., & Ilg, F. L. (1979). *Your six-year-old: Loving and defiant*. New York: Delta.

Ames, L. B., & Ilg, F. L. (1976). *Your three-year-old: Friend or enemy*. New York: Delta.

Armstrong, T. (1991). *Awakening your child's natural genius: Enhancing curiosity, creativity and learning ability*. Los Angeles: Tarcher.

Avery, C. (1993). *And with a light touch: Learning about reading, writing, and teaching with first graders*. Portsmouth, NH: Heinemann.

Bredekamp, S., & Rosegrant, T. (Eds.). (1992). *Reaching potentials: Appropriate curriculum and assessment for young children* (Vol. 1). Washington, DC: National Association for the Education of Young Children.

Bredekamp, S., & Rosegrant, T. (Eds.). (1995). *Reaching potentials: Transforming early childhood curriculum and assessment*. Washington, DC: National Association for the Education of Young Children.

Chaille, C., & Britain, L. (1997). *The young child as scientist: A constructivist approach to early childhood science education*. New York: Addison Wesley Longman.

Charney, R. (1997). *Teaching children to care: Management in the responsive classroom*. Greenfield, MA: Northeast Foundation for Children.

Christine, J., Roskos, K., Enz, B., Vukelich, C., & Newman, S. (1995). *Readings for linking literacy and play*. Newark, DE: International Reading Association.

Clay, M. (1993). *Reading recovery: A guidebook for teachers in training*. Portsmouth, NH: Heinemann.

Cochrane, O., & Cochrane, D. (1992). *Whole language evaluation for classrooms*. Winnipeg, Manitoba, Canada: Whole Language Consultants.

Diffily, D., & Morrison, K. (Eds.) (1996). *Family-friendly communication for early childhood programs*. Washington, DC: National Association for the Education of Young Children.

Dill, M., & Areglado, N. (1997). *Let's write*. New York: Scholastic.

Feldman, J. R. (1997). *Wonderful rooms where children can bloom!* Peterborough, NH: Crystal Springs Books.

Fisher, B. (1991). *Joyful learning*. Portsmouth, NH: Heinemann.

Fisher, B. (1995). *Thinking and learning together: Curriculum and community in a primary classroom*. Portsmouth, NH: Heinemann.

Fountas, I., & Pinnell, G. (1997). *Guided reading*. Portsmouth, NH: Heinemann.

Gardner, H. (1993). *Frames of mind: The theory of multiple intelligences*. New York: Basic.

Graves, M. (1989). *The teacher's idea book: Daily planning about the key experiences*. Ypsilanti, MI: Highscope Press.

Healy, J. M. (1990). *Endangered minds*. New York: Simon & Schuster.

Holt, B. (1977). *Science with young children*. Washington, DC: National Association for the Education of Young Children.

Ilg, F. (1985). *Scoring notes: The developmental examination*. New Haven, CT: Gesell Institute of Human Development.

Kellogg, R. (1969). *Analyzing children's art*. Palo Alto, CA: National Press.

Lewis, H. P. (Ed.). (1977). *Art for the preprimary child*. Reston, VA: National Art Education Association.

Lowenfeld, V., & Brittain, W. L. (1987). *Creative and mental growth*. New York: Macmillan.

National Board for Professional Teaching Standards. (1995, September). *Early Childhood/Generalist: Standards for National Board Certification*. Detroit, MI: Author.

Ostrow, J. (1995). *A room with a different view: First through third graders build community and create curriculum*. York, ME: Stenhouse.

Pinnell, G. S., & Fountas, I. C. (1997a). *A coordinator's guide to help America read*. Portsmouth, NH: Heinemann.

Pinnell, G. S., & Fountas, I. C. (1997b). *Help America read: A handbook for volunteers*. Portsmouth, NH: Heinemann.

Routman, R. (1989). *Transitions*. Portsmouth, NH: Heinemann.

Saul, W., & Jagusch, S. A. (Eds.). (1991). *Vital connections: Children, science, and books*. Portsmouth, NH: Heinemann.

Schwartz, S., & Pollishuke, M. (1991). *Creating the child-centered classroom*. New York: Owen.

Sheehan, K., & Waidner, M. (1991). *Earth child: Games, stories, activities, experiments, and ideas about living lightly on Planet Earth*. Tulsa, OK: Council Oak Books.

Smilansky, S., & Shefatya, L. (1990). *Facilitating play: A medium for promoting cognitive, socio-emotional, and academic development in young children*. Gaithersburg, MD: Psychosocial and Educational Publications.

Smutny, J. F., Walker, S. Y., & Meckstroth, E. A. (1997). *Teaching young gifted children in the regular classroom: Identifying, nurturing, and challenging ages 4–9*. Minneapolis, MN: Free Spirit Publishing, Emerging Literacy.

Strickland, D., & Morrow, L. (Eds.). (1989). *Young children learn to read and write*. Newark, DE: International Reading Association.

Wassermann, S. (1990). *Serious players in the primary classroom: Empowering children through active learning experiences*. New York: Teachers College Press.

APPENDIX 4.1
Child's Literacy Development: Parent Questionnaire
(Developed by Marlene Henriques)

In order to give a complete picture of the literacy development of your child, please complete the questionnaire below and return it to school. Thank you for your help.

Reading Behaviors

1. At what age did you introduce books to your child?
2. How often do you read with your child? (How many times a day or week?)

   a. Give examples of some of the recent books you've read with your child.
   b. How long do you read with your child at each sitting?
   c. Do you point to the words as you read?

Writing Behaviors

3. At what age did you introduce writing materials to your child?
4. Did you teach your child to write his or her name?
5. In what ways do you encourage your child to write at home? For example, do your encourage your child to draw pictures for or write to relatives?
6. Are writing materials readily available for your child to use as choice activities? What materials are available for writing at your home?

Oral Language

7. Do you and your child discuss the title of the book before reading? Do you discuss the book after you have read it?
8. Do you and your child watch television together and discuss the program?
9. Does your whole family generally eat dinner together? How many times per week?
10. Do you and your family play games together? What kinds and how often?
11. Have you taught your child the alphabet and the corresponding sounds of the letters?

APPENDIX 4.2
Assessing Literacy Development Using Multiple Strategies

Sample Responses: Anecdotal Records

One way candidates may monitor literacy development is by keeping anecdotal records of samples of the child's language. This practice provides important data that can be used to assess oral language development. For example, the reading specialist took anecdotal records of the child's speech patterns that revealed the student mixed up tenses and syntax and used double negatives. The teacher found that the student was stronger as a speaker than as a listener and provided examples from anecdotal records to document what happened when that student was given directions. For example, the student was able to verbalize something she had done. When the same language was used to give the student directions, she was unable to follow through with the task. The teacher used the English as a Second Language (ESL) teacher as a resource to gain information on effective strategies to use when giving ESL students oral directions. When the teacher utilized the ESL teacher's suggestions and repeated directions slowly and in different ways, giving the child ample time to translate them, she noted significant improvement in the student's ability to follow oral directions.

Demonstrating Literacy Development: Gathering Evidence

Samples Responses: Drawing and Writing

Candidates should consider the following: Can the child write his or her own name? In what stage of writing is this child (random letters, beginning sounds, etc.)? As the child moves to the next stage, gather artifacts to show this improvement. Analyze the child's drawings. Become familiar with the stages of children's drawings that coincide well with their literacy development. Is the child using the universal mandalas for a first drawing (just the circle for a head), or has she moved to the next stage, drawing the head-with-feet representation? Are there more details in the head than any other place? If so, then this is the part the child considers most important. Ask the child to draw a person and then count the number of parts (two arms count as one part) (Ilg, 1985, p. 49). The more parts represented usually indicates a higher level of cognitive thinking and corresponds well with literacy development.

APPENDIX 4.3
Introduction to Your Classroom Community

Activity 2: The Teaching Setting and the Characteristics of Children

Facilitators should be sure the candidates include a description of the diversity of their classroom community. Regarding the learning community, the candidate should be able to explain and answer the following: How do I establish a climate that fosters learning and sets norms for social interaction? How do the children interact, plan, and make decisions? Is my philosophy reflected in my classroom? Is my classroom designed to meet the wide range of developmental levels of the children?

Activity 3: Use of Space and Materials

The use of space and materials to enhance learning is the area in which the candidate explains the choice of materials, the room setup, and materials used to achieve the two overarching goals for the classroom community. Questions facilitators should encourage candidates to consider might include: Do changes take place in my classroom? How do the roles of the teacher and the children influence the environment? What is my approach to providing materials and learning activities? Why do I use these materials? Why do I arrange my room in this way? The answer may be as simple as the record player has to be in one area because that is where the electrical outlet is located and extension cords are not allowed in the room for safety reasons.

Sample Response: Relating to the Standards

The following example demonstrates how a candidate might respond in relation to the standards. A kindergarten teacher might discuss the math manipulatives she uses. These age-appropriate manipulatives might include Legos, links, unifix cubes, gears, puzzles, and pattern blocks, all of which could be located on low bookcases for easy access by the children (Standard I). The manipulatives are changed throughout the year to coincide with the themes studied and the increasing development of the children. The low bookcases are also used as dividers between four groups of trapezoid tables designated by different colors. This organization of tables with dividers encourages some privacy between the groups of tables, gives easy access to materials for those who finish their work, and discourages shouting between tables or running from one table to another (Standard II). It also helps the children function in a group (Goal 1-see Description sections regarding goals for this entry).

Activity 4: Rules and Routines

Rules and Routines is the third section of this entry. Facilitators should encourage candidates to discuss and reflect on the following questions: How do rules and routines help promote a sense of classroom community? How does change regarding rules and routines occur throughout the year? How are children involved in the changing rules and routines? How is family participation in supporting learning encouraged?

Activity 5: Reflecting on the Videotape

Reflection about the videotape has three sections that must be addressed: the event the candidate is videotaping, the significance of the event, and the evaluation.

Activity 5A: Videotape—Describing the Event

The facilitator should view the videotape with the candidate and discuss the following questions: What occurred directly before the taping? What is the actual event taking place? The candidate should include pertinent characteristics of specific students and any other information that will help the viewer understand the segment shown.

Activity 5B: Videotape—Significance of the Event

Discuss with the candidate how the videotape reflects ways he or she strives to meet the goals of this entry. The candidate must consider the following goals when addressing this section:

Goal 1: The children will display mutual respect, resolve conflicts, and develop social skills.
Goal 2: The children will show respect and appreciation for diversity.

Have candidates keep in mind questions such as: Are the children following the rules and routines and demonstrating the goals outlined above?

Activity 5C: Videotape—Evaluating the Learning

Facilitators should encourage candidates to discuss the successes and failures of the videotape. What would you change if you had to do it again? How could you make it better? What did you notice about the children during this viewing that you had not seen before? How did your voice sound? A typical entry might make note that the teacher was aware of those children with soft voices and asked Kristin to speak up and Calli to talk in a big voice. The teacher may note that she should have summarized more at the end by mentioning the various solutions again and asking the children to think about the one that would work best for them if they were in that situation.

An honest evaluation has more meaning and shows depth on the part of the teacher. See Hints for Videotaping: Technical Aspects and Videotaping: Analysis in the Introduction to Part II of this book for more helpful information.

Early Adolescence/Generalist

RICK WORMELI

Chapter 5 provides facilitators with:

- An overview of the EA/G portfolio entries.
- Assistance in planning activities for support sessions.
- Information about assessment center activities.
- A list of related resources.

CERTIFICATION CHARACTERISTICS

Applicants for Early Adolescence/Generalist (EA/G) certification are those who teach middle-school students (ages 11–15) in cross-disciplinary situations. This certification emphasizes significant and broad knowledge in multiple subject areas, but not necessarily expertise in those areas. Teachers seeking this certificate should have a solid base in inquiry learning and be willing to explore new knowledge with their students. This certificate is not intended for applicants who are primarily discipline-based, single-subject teachers; those teachers may do better by applying for a different certification field.

Among all the certification fields, the "Generalist" label creates the most confusion. A summary from the NBPTS's literature (EA/G, NBPTS Portfolio, 1997) clarifies the title well. An Early Adolescence/Generalist:

- Teaches across disciplines
- Plans teaching around substantive themes
- Has a broad knowledge of many subject areas
- Explores new territories
- Facilitates student inquiry.

Candidates who teach more than one subject, such as those in upper elementary levels, or who teach across disciplines at the secondary level, are good candidates for the generalist certification.

Although a generalist's foundation is one of inquiry and subject connections, it is important for him or her to have a basic core of knowledge from which to facilitate student learning. For a generalist, this means awareness of principles, concepts, skills, and terminology in the four core subjects (science, history/civics, English, and mathematics) and the arts (drawing, painting, sculpture, dance, music, singing, video, and film).

STANDARDS

The standards for EA/G certification are listed and described below (EA/G, NBPTS Portfolio, 1997). Facilitators must encourage candidates to become familiar with these standards and learn to recognize where they are addressed in the candidates' teaching practice:

Standard I: Knowledge of Young Adolescents

Accomplished generalists draw on their knowledge of early adolescent development and their relationships with students to understand and foster their students' knowledge, skills, interests, aspirations, and values.

Standard II: Knowledge of Content and Curriculum

Accomplished generalists draw on their knowledge of subject matter to establish goals and facilitate student learning within and across disciplines that comprise the middle grades curriculum.

Standard III: Instructional Resources

Accomplished generalists select, adapt, create, and use rich and varied resources.

Standard IV: Learning Environment

Accomplished generalists establish a caring, stimulating, inclusive, and safe community for learning where students can take intellectual risks and work independently and collaboratively.

Standard V: Meaningful Learning

Accomplished generalists require students to confront, explore, and understand important and challenging concepts, topics, and issues in purposeful ways.

Standard VI: Multiple Paths to Knowledge

Accomplished generalists use a variety of approaches to help students build knowledge and strengthen understanding.

Standard VII: Social Development

Accomplished generalists foster students' self-awareness, self-esteem, character, civic responsibility, and respect for diverse individuals and groups.

Standard VIII: Assessment

Accomplished generalists employ a variety of assessment methods to obtain useful information about student learning and development and to assist students in reflecting on their own progress.

Standard IX: Reflective Practice

Accomplished generalists regularly analyze, evaluate, and strengthen the effectiveness and quality of their practice.

Standard X: Family Partnerships

Accomplished generalists work with families to achieve common goals for the education of their children.

Standard XI: Collaboration with Colleagues

Accomplished generalists work with colleagues to improve schools and advance knowledge and practice in their field (NBPTS Portfolio, EA/G, 1997).

HINTS FOR FACILITATORS

✔ Read all materials candidates receive specific to this certification.

✔ Survey candidates to make sure they have chosen the area for which they best qualify.

CERTIFICATION FIELD ORGANIZER

The certification field organizer (Figure 5.1) provides an overview of the entire portfolio development and assessment center activities indicating where detailed information may be found about each entry. It is designed to assist a facilitator as he or she plans support sessions with candidates. It includes the following information about each entry:

- Entry title
- Standards that relate to the entry and should be specifically addressed by the candidate's entry
- Location from which candidate acquires data
- Facilitator hints specific to approximate time required for that entry
- Sample activities to assist facilitators working with candidates
- Related resources

This chapter provides details concerning all areas outlined in the grid.

	Portfolio entry	Standard	Hints	Sample activities	Resources
1	Writing as a Way of Knowing	Refer to Standards I, II, V, VIII, IX	—Article: "Coming to Know through Writing." —Writing as a tool not as an end.	—What's Everyone Else Doing? —Examine the Last Three —Graphic Organizer —Lesson Analysis —Active Prompts —Structured Self-Analysis —Literature Review	Publications on thinking, writing, creativity, intelligences, styles, and brain research (e.g., William Zinsser's works; see Resources at end of this chapter).
2	Exploring Connections to Mathematics	Refer to Standards I, II, V, VIII, IX	—NCTM, local organizations for integration ideas. —Math standards. —Get up to speed in math.	—What's Everyone Else Doing? —Examine the Last Three —Lesson Analysis —Structured Self-Analysis —Literature Review —Think Outside the Box —Making the Math Connection	Publications from National Council for Teachers of Mathematics at end of Chapter 7.
3	Thinking Together about a Social Issue	Refer to Standards I, II, V, VIII, IX	—Emphasize multiple perspectives. —Ease the video worry. —Up to speed in other subjects. —Up-to-date on current events.	—What Issue? —Choosing Groups —What's Everyone Else Doing? —Examine the Last Three —Lesson Analysis —Structured Self-Analysis —Literature Review —Conversation on Engagement —Videotape Analysis —Socratic Seminar —Sample Student Analysis	Publications and videos on thinking and discussions, see Resources at the end of this chapter (e.g., Jensen, 1995; Tredway, 1995).

	Portfolio entry	Standard	Hints	Sample activities	Resources
4	Engaging Students in Scientific Investigation	Refer to Standards I, II, V, VIII, IX	–Videotaping tips. –NSTA Standards. –Analysis of practice, not students. –Get the science right!	–What's Everyone Else Doing? –Examine the Last Three –Lesson Analysis –Structured Self-Analysis –Literature Review –Conversation on Engagement –Videotape Analysis –What Is Inquiry? –Excellent Inquiries –Excellent Class Discussions –Role Play –Sample Inquiry Experiences	Publications and videos on thinking, science skepticism, and science experiments; see Resources at the end of this chapter (e.g., Harvard–Smithsonian Center for Astrophysics, 1987; Hellman, 1998).
5 6	Document Accomplishments I, Professional Community Document Accomplishments II, Outreach to Families and Community	Refer to Standards III, X, XI	–Read, read, and read again all directions. –Practice responses and get feedback from group. –Start collecting verifications and documentation.	–What's Everyone Else Doing? –Draft Responses –Maintain Professional Portfolio –Discuss impact of work	Resources listed at end of this chapter.

	Description	Standards	Hints	Sample activities	Resources
Assessment Center	Logistics Assessments: Tests of Pedagogy	Refer to all Standards	–Stimulus materials sent in advance. –Group discussion: Clarify expectations, practice, revise thinking.	–Group Discussion: Coming to Know the Assessments and Making Responses to Them –Samples from Past Assessments	NBPTS materials sent in advance, candidate support group, resources listed for other chapters.

FIGURE 5.1. Certification Field Organizer: Early Adolescence/Generalist (EA/G).

CREATING EARLY ADOLESCENCE/GENERALIST PORTFOLIO ENTRIES

Entry 1: Writing as a Way of Knowing

Description

Successful EA/G candidates know that writing, reading, listening, and viewing are the ways through which we come to know all subjects. They see themselves as teachers and users of these processes in conjunction with their subject area's specific skills and content.

This entry asks candidates to show how they use writing in particular as a significant learning tool in their subject area. Specifically, this entry requests candidates to "demonstrate [their] use of writing for different purposes to develop student thinking in different settings and in response to different subjects and content exploration" (Entry 1, EA/G Portfolio, NBPTS, 1997).

Candidates examine this segment of their instructional practice by: (1) analyzing and assessing the written learning experiences of two students representing different challenges to the candidate, (2) analyzing three writing prompts the students make related to the candidate's goals for the students or objectives for the lesson, and (3) analyzing the use of writing in their classroom instructional delivery over a three- to four-week period.

It is important for candidates to choose student writing in which students incorporate specific content, insights, and appropriate structure. It is also important for candidates to briefly describe the context in which the piece is written: What is the unit of study? How does it connect to what preceded or what followed? Finally, it is important for candidates to describe how the student writing will be assessed: What will be the criteria? How were the criteria determined? How were they communicated to the student?

Standards to Be Addressed

Particular standards to be addressed in this entry are:

    Standard I: Knowledge of Young Adolescents
    Standard II: Knowledge of Subject Matter
    Standard V: Meaningful Learning
    Standard VIII: Assessment
    Standard IX: Reflective Practice

Hints for Facilitators

✔ The writing process gets to the heart of an EA/G and writing is key to its expression. For an in-depth look at this concept and its practical applications across subject areas, facilitators should read Wormeli's (1998) article, "Coming to Know through Writing." Facilitators could photocopy this article, distribute copies to the candidates, go over its main points with them, and urge them to study it themselves.

✔ William Zinsser's (1989) *Writing to Learn* offers a more comprehensive discussion of writing as a learning tool. He writes extensively on the use of writing as a way to come to know content and skills.

✔ Remind candidates that this entry advocates writing as a tool to teach and learn content and skills, not as an end in itself.

Activities for Assisting Candidates

ACTIVITY 1: ASSESSING NBPTS STANDARDS WITHIN ONE'S OWN PRACTICE

Activity 1A: What's Everyone Else Doing? Ask candidates to speak with colleagues about how they use writing as a tool with their students to promote better comprehension of their subjects.

Activity 1B. Examine the Last Three. Ask candidates to examine the last three writing assignments they gave their students and then determine to what extent those writing assignments fulfilled the scoring criteria for this assessment and documented the standards (as listed in the EA/G portfolio). If an assignment did not meet a standard, how might it be modified to do so? What would be a better alternative assignment next time?

Activity 1C. Lesson/Unit Analysis. Have candidates bring a lesson or unit to a support session and share its objectives and content. Then have fellow candidates brainstorm substantive writing experiences that would engage students and lead to mastery of the identified content. Also, discuss how the candidate would assess the effectiveness of those writing experiences.

ACTIVITY 2: WRITING AS A TOOL TO COME TO KNOW

Activity 2A. Active Prompts. To give candidates practice in the use of writing as a reflective tool, ask them to use *three* of the action verbs listed below as they write about any minitopic within their subject area (e.g., division of fractions, photosynthesis, effects of immigration on the Industrial Revolution, President Wilson's Fourteen Points, fractal patterns).

Action Verbs to Start Minitopic Writings

Analyze	Summarize	Explain
Construct	Decide between	Argue against
Why did	Argue for	Compare
Examine	Contrast	Modify
Identify	Plan	Classify
Critique	Define	Evaluate
Retell	Organize	Interpret
Interview	Expand	Find support for
Predict	Develop	Paraphrase
Categorize	Show	Criticize
Simplify	Deduce	Infer
Outline	Formulate	Blend
Suppose	Revise	Invent
Imagine	Devise	Compose
Combine	Rank	Recommend
Defend	Justify	Describe
Choose	Assess	Create

Once this is done, ask them to share what they noted about the process: How did one idea lead to another? Did use of the action words improve the writing? What would have been different had the assignment been simply to write about the minitopics? Did the act of writing about the minitopic compel the candidate to think analytically and in depth about the topic? Ask candidates to explain how such reflections done regularly could improve student comprehension and teacher assessment of students.

Activity 2B. Structured Self-Analysis. Ask candidates to write about their own practice for a period of two days. They can develop a structured self-analysis with such questions as the following:

What worked?
What didn't work?
What will I do differently tomorrow as a result of what happened today?
Whose needs are not being met?
How does this lesson fit into the larger picture?
Are the students building meaning for themselves or am I doing it for them?
Is this material meaningful to their lives or is it irrelevant?
How intellectually rigorous is this?
How can I tell the students are learning?
Were the students prepared for this lesson?
Why or why not?

After they have completed the previous assignment, ask candidates to reflect on how writing reflectively (describe, analyze, reflect) increases the quality of their self-analysis of practice, and what impact such reflection has on instructional decisions and the next day's lessons. It is important to assist candidates in understanding the difference between describing, analyzing and reflecting in their writing.

Activity 2C. Literature Review. In order to meet the needs of their diverse learners and demonstrate NBPTS standards, candidates will need a large repertoire of strategies in which writing is used as a tool for reflection and intellectual pursuit. Ask candidates to review the literature on writing-to-learn activities. See the Resources at the end of this chapter. You may want to have them maintain a running list or journal of such activities and share them at support meetings.

Entry 2: Exploring Connections to Mathematics

Description

In this entry, candidates present and analyze instructional experiences in which mathematics is used to study other disciplines, or in which the study of other disciplines leads to significant learning in mathematics. To do this, candidates analyze the responses of three students, each of whom presents a different instructional challenge to the candidate. These students *cannot* be the same ones used for any other portfolio entry.

The NBPTS is looking for experiences in which students "deepen and demonstrate" their knowledge of mathematics. Fifteen "Identify the three-dimensional shapes by the number of their vertices, edges, and faces," 20 decimal-to-percent conversions, or any list of computations by itself will not suffice. A debate over issues, comparison of fractal patterns and evolution, a persuasive essay, a student-produced video, a simulation, or creative bulletin board displays can easily require purposeful use of mathematics, as well as careful attention to numbers, percentages, and variables. Such activities demonstrate valid applications of mathematics across disciplines.

In their analysis of each student's work, candidates examine the extent to which the teaching assignments enabled students to make substantive connections to mathematics. Candidates will need to reflect on students' conceptions and misconceptions encountered in the lessons studied, and the extent to which students used math as a tool to come to know something else (or how they came to know math by studying another subject in which math was integrated). Teachers will also need to analyze the assessment and feedback they provided to their students during the lesson/unit of study.

Finally, candidates have to consider any revisions they would make to increase the success of the lesson or unit the next time they teach it. It is also important for candidates to briefly describe the context of the lesson or unit.

Standards to Be Addressed

The particular standards to be addressed for this entry are:

Standard I: Knowledge of Young Adolescents
Standard II: Knowledge of Subject Matter
Standard V: Meaningful Learning
Standard VIII: Assessment
Standard IX: Reflective Practice

Hints for Facilitators

✔ Candidates need to make sure their subject integrations are *purposeful*, that is, they promote new understanding in mathematics. Assigning a student the task of writing a paragraph chronicling the life of a famous mathematician probably will not result in new math insight. In contrast, a project in which a student interviews a building engineer about his use of mathematics on the job probably will lead to new mathematical understanding. Encourage generalist candidates to collaborate with their mathematics colleagues in the development of solid mathematics integration for this entry.

✔ Teachers of subjects not normally associated with mathematics must do purposeful lessons involving mathematics, not just math for demonstration's sake. This requirement might serve as a practical screening device for EA/G candidates because those teachers who must create such activities for the purposes of NBPTS certification may not truly be generalist teachers according to the definition offered at the beginning of this chapter. They might be better served by pursuing certification in their specific curriculum field. If the facilitator finds that the candidate feels his or her math background is less than expected for a NBPTS certified generalist teacher, then the facilitator should advise the candidate to spend time improving his or her grade-level math skills and grasp of concepts. While doing so, the candidate can pursue connections to other disciplines. The same is true of a math teacher who seeks additional discipline connections.

✔ The National Council of Teachers of Mathematics (NCTM), local math organizations, and colleagues are helpful allies in identifying examples of successful math integration.

✔ It is essential that candidates be familiar with the national math standards from the NCTM. These standards call for cross-discipline approaches, some of which are published with demonstration activities. Urge candidates to read them, for they can spark ideas for lessons and reflection. Demonstrating knowledge of these standards and how they manifest in one's practice speaks well of a candidate's professionalism.

Activities for Assisting Candidates

ACTIVITY 1: ASSESSING NBPTS STANDARDS WITHIN ONE'S OWN PRACTICE

Activity 1A. What's Everyone Else Doing? Ask candidates to speak with colleagues about how they use mathematics as a tool with their students to promote their learning of other disciplines.

Activity 1B. Examine the Last Three. Ask candidates to examine their last three assignments in which mathematics was integrated with other subjects. They should determine to what extent those math-related assignments fulfilled the scoring criteria for this assessment (as listed in the EA/G portfolio). If a piece did not meet the standard, how might it be modified to do so? What would be a better alternative assignment for next time?

Activity 1C. Lesson/Unit Analysis. Ask candidates who teach English, science, history, or the arts to bring a lesson plan or unit plan to a support session and share its content and objectives. Then ask the presenter's fellow candidates to brainstorm substantive math experiences that would engage students and lead to mastery of the identified content. Finally, encourage the presenter to assess the effectiveness of those suggested math experiences as a way to teach the content of the lesson(s).

ACTIVITY 2: ACTIVITIES WITH CONNECTIONS TO MATHEMATICS

Activity 2A. Structured Self-Analysis. Ask candidates to write about their math integration for one week. They can do a structured self-analysis, asking themselves such questions as:

What math is being learned?
What misconceptions are still evident?
What worked?
What didn't work?
What will I do differently tomorrow as a result of what happened today?
Whose needs are not being met?
How does this lesson fit into the larger picture?
Are the students building meaning for themselves or am I doing it for them?
Is this material useful to their lives?
How intellectually rigorous is this material?
How can I tell the students are learning?
Were the students prepared for this lesson?
Why or why not?

Activity 2B. Literature Review. In order to meet the needs of their diverse learners and demonstrate NBPTS standards, candidates will need a large repertoire of strategies in which mathematics is a tool for learning. Ask candidates to review the literature on mathematics integration with other subjects.

Encourage candidates to maintain a running list or journal of such activities and ask them to share their new ones at support meetings. (See Wormeli, 1998, for some good ideas about writing and math connections.)

Activity 2C. Think Outside the Box. Working on this entry may open some candidates' eyes to possibilities they never saw before. To enhance the development of cross-discipline connections, conduct activities in which candidates are forced to think unconventionally for a while.

Activities can come in many forms, including problem solving, role playing, puzzles, what-if scenarios, collaboration, and artistic expression. Once the candidates creative juices are flowing, then lead discussions on possible math–subject connections.

Debono's (1985) "Plus-Minus-Interesting" and "BCCQ Quadrant" and Kriegel's (1991) "Making the Mathematics Connection" are three excellent activities to encourage further discussion about mathematics.

Entry 3: Thinking Together about a Social Issue

Description

Students in an EA/G's class work with cross-discipline activities, address substantive themes, explore new territories, and ask lots of questions. This entry's group inquiry into a social issue is a perfect structure to enable true generalists to shine. This activity is very similar to the science inquiry labs required in the science certification areas.

In this entry the candidate selects a group of four to six students who are engaged in discussion of a substantive social or historical theme or issue. The candidate facilitates the students' questions about the topic and their pursuit of answers to those questions. The interaction is recorded on an *unedited* 20-minute videotape, whose content the candidate must describe, analyze, and reflect upon in writing.

The written commentary on the videotape should describe the individuals who were selected for the group, how the candidate facilitated student-directed discussion and learning, how the chosen topic encouraged the exploration of multiple perspectives and connections to the students' lives, and how the student responses to the topic encouraged the students' own questions.

Candidates must discuss the level of success of the inquiry discussion and their own role in that level of success. They need to consider the value of using the small group inquiry approach to teach this particular set of multiple perspectives. They must target the work of two students for special analysis, and demonstrate an ability to accurately diagnose where the students stand developmentally and to determine the students' understanding of the topic presented. In addition, they must reflect on how their assignment "accommodated the intellectual curiosity and needs" (Entry 3, EA/G Portfolio, NBPTS, 1997) of the students. The total written commentary is to be no longer than 12 pages.

Standards to Be Addressed

The standards to be addressed for this entry include:

Standard I: Knowledge of Young Adolescents
Standard II: Knowledge of Subject Matter
Standard V: Meaningful Learning
Standard VIII: Assessment
Standard IX: Reflective Practice

Hints for Facilitators

✔ Make sure candidates understand that assessors will be looking for the extent to which the chosen learning experiences facilitate exploration of multiple perspectives. The assessors will also be looking at how the candidate promotes that exploration and makes it relevant to students' lives.

✔ Most candidates are concerned about this portfolio entry because it must be videotaped. Put their mind at ease. Review and share with them all the hints on videotaping offered in the Introduction to Part II of this book. Then encourage the candidates to make practice tapings. When shown for and discussed with the other candidates, these first practice tapes will yield clear procedures for successful taping.

✔ Regarding the videotape, remind the candidate that both he or she and his or her students must be audible on the tape. Candidates have been unsuccessful in this entry simply because assessors have not been able to hear the teacher and/or the students. Remind candidates to pay particular attention to setting up microphones and to tape very close to the action.

✔ Also regarding taping, make sure the camera focuses on the faces of the students. Assessors comment that seeing students' faces helps them judge the impact of a teacher's lesson on student learning. Candidates, too, need to appear on screen some of the time, but not more than half the time, because the focus is on student-directed discussion as facilitated (not necessarily led) by the candidate.

✔ Advise candidates to do many tapings over several weeks so they have plenty of segments from which to choose for their final submission.

✔ If the candidate feels that his or her background in other key cross-disciplinary subjects is less than expected for a NBPTS certified generalist teacher, then he or she should spend time increasing skills and knowledge in those subject areas. In the course of doing so, connections to other disciplines can be pursued.

✔ Candidates need to be up-to-date on current events and thinking with regard to the identified social issues.

Activities for Assisting Candidates

ACTIVITY 1: ASSESSING NBPTS STANDARDS WITHIN ONE'S OWN PRACTICE

Activity 1A. What Issue to Choose? The social issues candidates choose to examine in this entry need to incorporate more than one discipline. When several candidates share, such sharing provides multiple perspectives on each issue. Modern issues should be relevant to students' lives, for example, censoring rap lyrics, no smoking ordinances, racism, compulsory education, wearing hats in school, or age requirements on the right to vote.

To get the ideas flowing about which topic to choose, have candidates list important social or historical issues that students will (or might) encounter in the course of study for the next few weeks. (Some ideas to begin the discussion can be found in Appendix 5.1 at the end of this chapter.) Again, brainstorming with a colleague is highly recommended.

When they have generated an initial list, have them study the list and circle the topics whose investigations would require multiple perspectives. Of those circled, ask candidates which ones lend themselves to having students pose and pursue their own inquiries related to the issues. Finally, ask candidates to choose issues from this narrowed list that they feel confident in facilitating with small student groups.

Notice you're asking them to choose *issues* and not *one issue*. Candidates must facilitate and videotape multiple small groups and multiple discussions within those groups. Candidates will want choice in what they submit.

Activity 1B. Choosing Discussion Groups. Candidates must exercise forethought in choosing the students to constitute a small group. Thus facilitators should lead a discussion on what makes for a successful early adolescent grouping, how to teach group discussion skills to students, and how to get all group members to contribute. Some group structures work better than others, depending on the goal of the group activity. Have candidates discuss different structuring arrangements for groups and their advantages and disadvantages.

Remind candidates that this entry requires an analysis of practice, not an examination of the level of student performance. Choosing groups consisting of exceptionally productive or academically proficient students is not always the best plan. Such students are likely to learn *in spite of* the candidate. Instead, it might be better to choose students for whom the candidate's coaching will make the difference in their learning. These students' responses and the candidate's subsequent analysis of their work and his or her own practice will more dramatically express the standards at work in the candidate's classroom.

Activity 1C. What's Everyone Else Doing? Ask candidates to speak with colleagues about how they use small groups and student inquiry to study multiple perspectives on social issues. Have them interview several colleagues and report back to the support group.

Activity 1D. Examine the Last Three. Ask candidates to examine the last three assignments in which small-group discussions were used as teaching tools. They can determine the extent to which those discussions fulfilled the scoring criteria for this assessment (as listed in the EA/G portfolio). If a discussion did not meet the standard, how might it be modified to do so? What would be a better alternative assignment for next time?

Activity 1E. Lesson/Unit Analysis. Ask each candidate to present a model lesson on a social issue that might likely involve student-directed learning and discussion. Then have fellow candidates brainstorm substantive social issue experiences that would engage students and lead to mastery of content. Finally, ask the presenting candidate to assess the effectiveness of those experiences and define the role he or she would play in the experience.

ACTIVITY 2: LEADING STUDENT INQUIRIES AND DISCUSSIONS

Activity 2A. Conversation on Engagement. The facilitator should ask candidates to discuss their strategies for promoting successful group explorations of social issues. Make sure to explore how, once the issue has been initiated, the teacher steps back and allows the students to explore its many aspects. The facilitator should encourage the candidates to share how they engage the students, manage the learning, assess student understanding, and keep students participating.

Activity 2B. Videotape Discussion and Analysis. Have candidates videotape samples of classroom discussions—anything from 5 minutes to 20 minutes—and bring these samples in for discussion. As a group, analyze these sample discussions and the teacher's role in them using the scoring criteria found in the EA/G portfolio instructions. Ask candidates: What worked? What didn't work? What would he or she do differently the next time? The facilitator could provide videotape samples in which the camera person did not heed the videotaping instructions and then lead a discussion in which candidates suggest how to improve these flawed videotapes.

Activity 2C. Structured Self-Analysis. Ask candidates to write about their social studies integration for a period of two days. Encourage them to do a structured self-analysis in which they address such questions as the following:

What social studies is being learned?

What misconceptions are still evident?

What worked?

What didn't work?

What will I do differently tomorrow as a result of what happened today?

Whose needs are not being met?

How does this lesson fit into the larger picture?

Are the students building meaning for themselves or am I doing it for them?

Is this material something useful to their lives?

How intellectually rigorous is this material?

How can I tell the students are learning?

Were the students prepared for this lesson?

Why or why not?

Activity 2D. Literature Review. In order to meet the needs of their diverse learners and demonstrate NBPTS standards, candidates will need a large repertoire of strategies with which to engage students, facilitate student-directed discussions, and assess student learning in small group discussions. Ask candidates to review the literature on small-group facilitation for early adolescence. You may want to have them maintain a running list or journal of the ideas they glean from the literature and to share at support meetings.

Activity 2E. Socratic Seminar. Content is internalized and retained for the long term with activities in which students talk to each other and apply what's learned to new situations. A Socratic Seminar is a highly effective learning vehicle, for students speak 97% of the class time and the teacher 3%. Not designed for the presentation of facts, a Socratic Seminar is used more for *applying* knowledge than *gathering* it. It is one of many ways to structure student exploration of a social issue. Candidates may wish to give it a try and reflect on its success with their candidate group. Tredway (1995) explains how to conduct a Socratic Seminar.

ACTIVITY 3: PRACTICING WRITTEN ANALYSIS

The facilitator might ask candidates to read the Sample Analysis of a teacher's observation found in Appendix 5.2, at the end of this chapter. Candidates would benefit from highlighting the sections of the sample that illustrate "reporting" (description) and "interpreting" (analysis).

Candidates probably need to practice analysis of their targeted students and their work. The sample is an excerpt of one teacher's observations of one student and offers a first attempt at analyzing students and their work. Practicing this process on an ongoing basis is important for all candidates and will be useful in all entries. Answering the required questions listed in the EA/G NBPTS portfolio directions is a good place to start when beginning student analysis.

Entry 4: Engaging Students in Scientific Investigation

Description

Constructivist in nature, this entry requires candidates to demonstrate how they assist young adolescents as they learn to engage in scientific inquiry to enhance their understanding of a selected topic (Entry 4, EA/G Portfolio, NBPTS, 1997). The entry requires the candidate to identify a concept or issue to be investigated (which may or may not be in the science curriculum), to present it to his or her students, and to facilitate student use of the scientific method or a similar inquiry method in their exploration of the topic.

Students must demonstrate the gathering, managing, and interpretation of empirical data. They will develop hypotheses, conduct experiments (or gather data, e.g., through a survey), and draw conclusions. The candidate who is not a science teacher shouldn't worry: the scientific process is applicable to all subject areas.

This entry is an excellent integration of all that makes a generalist a generalist.

Science provides context and meaning for the teaching of many disciplines. It is important for candidates to truly understand the content they present. Such understanding should come through clearly in the whole-class discussion (documented via a 20-minute videotape), the written commentary (no more than 10 pages), and the instructional artifact presented as evidence of the candidate's knowledge of pertinent facts and concepts.

The entry involves the choice of an instructional artifact, such as an object, experience, or prompt, that gives students something to talk about for 20 minutes, or that demonstrates significant evidence of worthwhile learning subsequent to the discussion.

Candidates must plan formative and summative assessments that demonstrate their knowledge of early adolescents and the subject matter, as well as accurately diagnose student conceptions and misconceptions.

The written commentary also asks candidates to explain how the topic was chosen, how it was introduced, and how it relates to previous learning. Candidates will have to explain the nature of the questions and discussions:

Who said what and when?
Was it student-driven or teacher-driven?
What was the candidate's role in the discussion?
How did the candidate accommodate different learners?
What does the tone and structure of the discussion say about the candidate's classroom environment?

In the evaluation section, candidates explain what worked and what didn't, how the discussions illuminated student perceptions for the candidate, and how the discussion impacted future lessons. Candidates will also have to comment on the effect of the instructional artifact on student learning.

Standards to Be Addressed

The standards to be addressed for this entry include:

Standard I: Knowledge of Young Adolescents
Standard II: Knowledge of Subject Matter
Standard V: Meaningful Learning
Standard VIII: Assessment
Standard IX: Reflective Practice

Hints for Facilitators

✔ Facilitators may want to arrange a collaboration with a science teacher colleague to discuss the possibilities for cross-discipline integration.

✔ Candidates should be advised to choose a topic they know well. A comprehensive working knowledge base will make it easier for them to draw connections and facilitate student learning.

✔ Remind candidates that the concepts and issues to investigate should have relevance for the students. Relevant topics generate more student participation than other less-immediate topics; moreover, they demonstrate a candidate's knowledge of students and their development. The learning should be substantive, connected to the real world, not done just for show.

✔ Facilitators should define "artifact." Examples of stimulus artifacts include news articles, presentation of a community issue, classroom demonstrations, video excerpts, stories, and simulations. Postdiscussion evidence of worthwhile learning includes anything in which students apply knowledge gained through the whole-class discussion to other situations: follow-up experiments, findings used in other discussions, writings, exhibitions, and successful peer coaching.

✔ Remind candidates about the videotaping advice you offered in regard to Entry 3. The same advice applies in Entry 4, except in this case the taped discussion will involve the whole class, not a small group.

✔ Facilitators should remind candidates that the topic they choose must be something that can be effectively taught in science inquiry experiences. For instance, conducting experiments to learn more about three-dimensional (3-D) solids may be an interesting tangential idea, but not the primary tool for student understanding of 3-D solids.

✔ Stress the idea that the best inquiries come from a sincere interest in wanting to answer a question and then designing and implementing the methodology to search for that answer. Successful inquiry starters include:

- How can _____ stay afloat?
- What effect will _____ have on _____?
- Why does _____ happen?
- What's the pattern of _____?
- Under what conditions would _____ happen?
- Is there a way to _____?
- What's the proof that _____?

✔ The National Science Teachers Association (NSTA) standards are an excellent source of ideas for using scientific investigation. They provide rational, proper terminology and specific activities related to this exact endeavor. Encourage your candidates to read and discuss those standards and their elaborations.

✔ As with Entry 3, remind candidates that Entry 4 is an analysis of practice, not a look at the level of student performance. Exceptionally productive or academically proficient classes of students will not always show a candidate's talents as an accomplished teacher. It might be more revealing to choose students for whom the candidate's guidance will make the difference in their learning. These students' responses and the candidate's subsequent analysis of their work and practice will more dramatically express the standards at work in the candidate's practice.

✔ Facilitator should remind candidates that as generalists working with science investigations, they must "get the science right" and not perpetuate any misconceptions. Candidates must make sure they understand the concepts and terms themselves, and make frequent checks for student understanding.

✔ Candidates will benefit greatly from viewing the video *A Private Universe* (Annenberg/CPB Math and Science Collection, 1995), which highlights the long-term effects of misconceptions about science (see Resources for ordering information).

Activities for Assisting Candidates

ACTIVITY 1: ASSESSING NBPTS STANDARDS WITHIN ONE'S OWN PRACTICE

Activity 1A. What's Everyone Else Doing? Ask candidates to speak with colleagues about how they use whole-class discussion and science inquiry experiences to study topics.

Activity 1B. Examine the Last Three. Ask candidates to examine the last three assignments in which whole-class discussions and/or science inquiry were used as teaching tools. They should determine to what extent those strategies fulfilled the scoring criteria for this assessment. If a discussion or an inquiry did not meet the standard, how might it be modified to do so? What would be a better alternative assignment for next time?

Activity 1C. Lesson/Unit Analysis. Have a candidate present content and skills for a particular lesson that involves whole-class discussion and science inquiry experiences. Then have fellow candidates brainstorm what the lesson would look like. Ask them to address these questions: How would students be engaged? How would such engagement lead to mastery of the identified content? What would students have to know ahead of time in order to be successful with the lesson? Discuss how the candidate would assess the effectiveness of those experiences and define the role he or she would play in the experiences. Finally, compare the group's brainstormed lesson against the standards and scoring rubric for this entry.

Activity 1D. Show the Video A Private Universe *(Annenberg/CPB Math and Science Collection, 1995).* This video can spark candidates' self-examination of their instruction and assessment practices. Pose the following questions: How do accomplished teachers know students are learning what they intend for them to learn? How do they check for understanding, and how do they correct for misunderstanding? How do accomplished teachers know the science concepts they are teaching are accurate?

ACTIVITY 2: LEADING STUDENT INQUIRIES AND DISCUSSIONS

Activity 2A. Conversation on Engagement. Ask candidates to discuss the strategies for successful large-group inquiry experiences. Focus discussion by using the following questions: How does an accomplished teacher conduct them? How does the teacher engage the students, manage the learning, assess student understanding, and keep students moving toward their goal?

Activity 2B. Videotape Discussion and Analysis. Encourage candidates to videotape whole-class discussions—in segments ranging from 5–20 minutes—and bring these segments in for group viewing and discussion. (See Entry 3, Activity 2.B.)

Activity 2C. Structured Self-Analysis. Ask candidates to write about their inquiry experiences. They can do a structured self-analysis using the same questions listed in Entry 3, Activity 2.C.

Activity 2D. Literature Review. Ask candidates to review the literature on whole-group facilitation for early adolescence. Point out that they will benefit from keeping a running list or journal of good ideas they discover in their reading. Encourage candidates to share these ideas at support meetings.

Activity 2E. What Is Inquiry? EA/G candidates need to take time to understand what is an inquiry experience and what is not an enquiry experience. Lead the candidates in creating a common definition of inquiry. Salient attributes that candidates should address include: The teacher facilitates *student-generated* questions to investigate, rather than telling students what to study. The investigation's procedures are also designed by students, rather than being spelled out in recipe form by the teacher. Consequently, any investigation in which students simply validate results set forth by the teacher is not considered a true inquiry.

In a true inquiry experience, the end result is unknown to the students. The teacher's role is to ask those questions that spark interest and guide curious (and safe) exploration of the topic.

After creating the group definition, the facilitator should spend some time with candidates exploring possible inquiry experiences that use science and its methods in order to understand a topic.

Activity 2F. Share Excellent Inquiries. Encourage the candidates to find and share excellent inquiry lessons (videotaped or transcribed) in which science investigation played an important role in student understanding of a larger topic. Have the group list the successful attributes of the lessons and link these to the agreed-upon definition.

Activity 2G. Share Excellent Class Discussions. Ask the candidates to find and share videotapes of teachers engaged in highly successful whole-group discussions in which the teachers are facilitating student exploration of a topic, rather than telling them what to think. In group session, have the candidates brainstorm a list of teacher techniques. These include facilitating discussion, rather than lecturing; posing challenging questions; providing wait time for student responses; giving effective feedback to student responses; giving silent students opportunities to participate; and providing encouragement and an emotionally safe atmosphere for open discussion.

Activity 2H. Role Play. Role-play scenarios similar to ones candidates encounter in their own classrooms. Give each candidate an opportunity to lead a discussion on a topic of interest, with the ultimate goal being to identify a question to investigate and a procedure by which the candidate may pursue it.

ACTIVITY 3: SAMPLE SCIENCE INQUIRY EXPERIENCES

Examples from *In Search of Understanding: The Case for Constructivist Classrooms* (Brooks & Brooks, 1993) can be used to generate meaningful discussion. We especially recommend Learning Photosynthesis (p. 19), From a Library to the Periodic Table of the Elements (pp. 50–52), Salmon Lifestyles (p. 77), and From Things to Gods (p. 80). Some of these exercises are not complete inquiry experiences; have your candidate group discuss each one and then describe what it would take to make it a full inquiry experience.

Entries 5 and 6: Documented Accomplishments

Description

The focus of these entries is on those parts of a highly accomplished teacher's practice that take place outside the classroom. In addition, candidates get to demonstrate their contributions to the profession and to family–school–community partnerships. The facilitator should stress that candidates must enable assessors to see the significance of those contributions, not just list them.

There are two sections in this component, Entry 5: Collaboration in the Professional Community, and Entry 6: Outreach to Families and Community. Each section is subdivided into three areas, candidates need to choose two of these areas for their response, which is an interpretive summary of their work in that area. The first area under Outreach to Families and Community is required. Although the NBPTS expects candidates to provide ample evidence of their contributions outside the classroom (and their significance), the candidate must adhere to strict page limits.

Under Collaborations in the Professional Community portion, candidates choose from three areas on which to reflect and provide evidence for their significant contributions:

1. Development or review of instructional resources and/or practices
2. Educational policy and practices through work in professional organizations and settings
3. Collaborative work with colleagues in developing pedagogy, as a mentor or a learner.

For each area, candidates describe their activities and why those chosen examples provide strong evidence of accomplishment. As evidence, the NBPTS is looking for letters of attestation or verification, as well as tangible products such as conference brochures, published articles/books, or developed curriculum materials (none of which can be more than five years old).

Entry 6, Outreach to Families and Community, is structured the same way. Candidates explain the work in which they were involved, including the role they played. It is vital for candidates to examine the impact of their work on students, their families, and the community at large. The required area under this section asks candidates to demonstrate how they "created ongoing interactive communication with families and other adults interested in students' progress and learning." Candidates need to choose one area for response from the remaining two areas:

- Demonstrate consistent effort to understand parents' concerns about student learning, subject matter, and curriculum.
- Connect the school program to community needs/resources/interests.

Standards to Be Addressed

Entries 5 and 6 address three standards:

Standard III: Instructional Resources
Standard X: Family Partnerships
Standard XI: Collaboration with Colleagues

Hints for Facilitators

✔ The portfolio descriptions for this entry frequently use the phrase "convincing and substantial evidence of sustained or significant contribution" (EA/G Portfolio, NBPTS, 1997). Advise candidates to clarify what is meant by this in each area.

✔ Point out that what constitutes "evidence" is largely up to the candidates. Past examples from successful candidates include notes to parents, curriculum, contact logs, articles, workshop outlines, letters, and newly designed assessments.

Activities for Assisting Candidates

ACTIVITY 1: DRAFT RESPONSES

Ask candidates to do the write-ups according to the portfolio directions and share them with the support group. Group members should assess a fellow candidate's response in terms of the standards listed for this entry and the criteria listed in the portfolio directions.

ACTIVITY 2: ESTABLISH PROFESSIONAL PORTFOLIOS

Ask candidates to start and maintain a professional portfolio for the duration of the NBPTS certification process. Have them collect evidence of highly accomplished practice for the past five years. Before they begin this task, however, help the group brainstorm to determine what makes for good artifacts of accomplished practice. Many successful candidates have chosen to use expandable files for gathering such information, but any organized method will work.

ACTIVITY 3: DISCUSS IMPACT

It is often easier to list one's professional activities than to explain how those activities impact students, families, and communities. Success for this entry will come not in the mere listing of contributions, but in how well the candidate explains the positive impact of those contributions on the students, families, and community. The facilitator should lead a discussion in which candidates focus on how particular professional activities impact stakeholders. Candidates are often pleasantly surprised to discuss just how much positive impact they really have.

ACTIVITY 4: WHAT'S EVERYONE ELSE DOING?

Ask candidates to speak with colleagues about how they contribute and measure the impact of their contributions.

ASSESSMENT CENTER PREPARATION

Description

To participate in the second part of the NBPTS assessment process, standardized assessments at a testing center, candidates report to a Sylvan Learning Center by appointment on any day from approximately mid-June through mid-August. There, they undergo four, 90-minute assessments, with breaks between assessments, which makes for an 8-hour day. Facilitators should make sure candidates understand assessment center rules. Candidates may use the center's word processors to take the assessments or they may write their responses by hand. Candidates are allowed to bring printed materials such as dictionaries and notes, but all printed materials must be turned in with the assessments; none are returned to the candidate. Math tools, such as calculators, however, are returned to the candidate. Candidates must bring photo identification, plenty of pens and pencils, and any notes or materials the assessment stimulus booklets suggest.

Standards to Be Addressed

All of the standards for the certification field are relevant to the responses at the assessment center.

Hints for Facilitators

✔ The assessments are a test of the candidates' pedagogy: knowledge of content area and of how to teach it. They are not tests of writing ability.

✔ Stimulus materials will be sent in advance to facilitate preparation by candidates.

✔ Bulleted lists or phrases are acceptable responses.

Activities for Assisting Candidates

Activity 1: Review of Advance Materials

The facilitator should arrange for the candidate and his or her support group to go over each assessment in the materials sent to the candidate by the NBPTS. Before the assessment, the candidate should:

- Clarify directions for expectations of the assessment.
- Understand the standards that must be demonstrated for each assessment.
- Brainstorm possible responses to the prompts.
- Incorporate *all* considerations as listed in the prompt (e.g., "How does this activity meet the unique needs of your students?" is a common question candidates must answer).
- Prepare any and all notes allowed during the actual assessment, as dictated by the advance materials.
- Complete additional reading and discussion in particular areas of practice if the candidate feels anxious or unprepared after reviewing the materials.

Candidates must respond completely to all prompts. It would be beneficial for each member of the support group to practice sharing their responses, then have the group members paraphrase their interpretation of what the candidate said, offering areas for improvement.

Activity 2: Examine Past Assessments

The assessments at the center change over time. Nonetheless, candidates can prepare themselves by examining past assessments. They'll get a sense of the kind of thinking and standards demonstrations that the NBPTS requires. Sample assessment center prompts are found in the assessment center materials from the NBPTS.

RESOURCES

Allen, S. (1998). *Dumbth: The lost art of thinking.* Amherst, NY: Prometheus.
Armstrong, T. (1994). *Multiple intelligences in the classroom.* Alexandria, VA: Association for Supervision and Curriculum Development.

Atwell, N. (1990). *Coming to know: Writing to learn in the intermediate grades.* Portsmouth, NH: Heinemann.

Beane, J. A. (1997). *Curriculum integration: Designing the core of democratic education.* New York: Teachers College Press.

De Bono, E. (1985). *Six thinking hats.* Boston: Little, Brown.

Brooks, J. G., & Brooks, M. G. (1993). *In search of understanding: The case for constructivist classrooms.* Alexandria, VA: Association for Supervision and Curriculum Development. (To order, call 1-800-933-2723.)

Canady, R. L., & Rettig, M. D. (1996). *Teaching in the block.* Princeton, NJ: Eye on Education. (To order, call 1-609-395-0005.)

Frank, M. (1979). *If you're trying to teach kids how to write, you've gotta have this book!* Nashville, TN: Incentive Publications.

Graham, S., & Rogers, S. (1998). *The high performance tool box: Succeeding with performance tasks, projects, and assessments.* Evergreen, CO: Peak Learning Systems. (Also available on-line at: www.peaklearn.com)

Harrison, A. F., & Bramson, R. M. (1984). *The art of thinking.* New York: Berkley.

Harvard–Smithsonian Center for Astrophysics. (1987). *A private universe* [Videotape]. (Available from Annenberg/CPB Math and Science Collection, S. Burlington, VT)

   From its famous opening scene at a Harvard graduation, this classic of educational research brings into sharp focus the dilemma facing all educators: Why don't even the brightest students truly grasp basic science concepts? This award-winning program traces the problem with interviews of eloquent Harvard graduates and professors to Heather, a bright middle-school student who has some strange ideas about the orbits of the planets. (To order, call 1-800-965-7373; or write: Annenberg/CPB Math and Science Collection, P.O. Box 2345, S. Burlington, VT 05407-2345.)

Hellman, H. (1998). *Great feuds in science: Ten of the liveliest disputes ever.* New York: Wiley.

Jensen, E. (1995). *Super teaching.* Del Mar, CA: Turning Point Publishing. (To order, call 1-800-325-4769 or 1-619-755-6670; or on-line at: www.thebrainstore.com.)

Kriegel, R. (1991). *If it ain't broke, break it! and other unconventional wisdom for a changing business world.* New York: Warner Books.

Lavoie, R. D.(1989). *How difficult can this be? A learning disabilities workshop* [Videotape]. (Available from WETA Video, Ho-Ho-Kus, NJ)

   This unique program allows viewers to experience the same frustration, anxiety, and tension that children with learning disabilities face in their daily lives. Teachers, social workers, psychologists, parents, and friends who have participated in Richard Lavoie's workshop reflect upon their experience and the way it changed their approach to children with learning disabilities. (To order, call 1-800-343-5540; fax: 201/652-1973; or write: WETA Video, 22-D Hollywood Ave., Ho-Ho-Kus, NJ 07423.)

Marzano, R. J. (1992). *A different kind of classroom: Teaching with dimensions of learning.* Alexandria, VA: Association for Supervision and Curriculum Development. (To order, call 1-703-549-9110.)

McCarthy, B. (1987). *The 4MAT system.* Barrington, IL: Excel.

Murphy, P., & Shimek, S. (1991). *The Exploratorium science snackbook: Teacher-created versions of Exploratorium exhibits.* San Francisco: Exploratorium Teacher Institute. (To order, call The Exploratorium, San Francisco, 1-800-359-9899.)

National Board for Professional Teaching Standards. (1997). *Early adolescence/generalist portfolio.* San Antonio, TX: Psychological Corporation/Harcourt Brace & Company. (To order, call 1-800-22-TEACH.)

National Council of Teacher of Mathematics. (1989). *Curriculum and evaluation standards for school mathematics.* Reston, VA: Author.

National Research Council. (1996). *National Science Education Standards*. Washington, DC: National Academy Press. (To order, call 1-800-624-6242, or 1-202-334-3313 in the Washington metropolitan area; order on-line at http://www.nap.edu/nap/online/nses/order.html; view via the Internet at: http://www.nap.edu/nap/online/nses.)

Parks, S., & Black, H. (1990). *Book II: Organized thinking*. Pacific Grove, CA: Critical Thinking Press and Software. (To order, call 1-800-458-4849.)

Rief, L. (1992). *Seeking diversity*. Portsmouth, NH: Heinemann.

Sagan, C. (1996). *The demon-haunted world: Science as candle in the dark*. New York: Ballantine Books.

Saphier, J., & Gower, R. (1987). *The skillful teacher*. Carlisle, MA: Research for Better Teaching.

Schurr, S. L. (1994) *Dynamite in the classroom: A how-to book for teachers*. Columbus, OH: National Middle School Association. (To order, call 1-800-528-6672.)

Spandel, V., & Stiggins, R. (1997). *Creating writers: Linking assessment and instruction*. New York: Longman.

Sylwester, R. (1995). *A celebration of neurons: An educator's guide to the human brain*. Alexandria, VA: Association for Supervision and Curriculum Development. (To order, call 1-703-549-9110; or write Dr. Sylwester at College of Education, University of Oregon.)

Tredway, L. (1995). Socratic seminar: Engaging students in intellectual discourse. *Educational Leadership, 53*(1), 26–29.

Wormeli, R. (1998, Spring). "Coming to know through writing: Student scientists, artists, mathematicians, and historians as writers." *Crucial Link* (Virginia Middle School Association magazine), pp. 8–9, 25–30.

Since writing is really teaching readers what one knows, and teaching someone else is one of the best ways to learn content, the author makes the argument that writing is a highly effective instructional strategy in science, history, and mathematics. Inspired by several excerpts from William Zinsser's Writing to Learn, Wormeli provides a rationale for developing writing activities in content areas, making the case that writing is a thinking activity more than a grammar activity.

Zinsser, W. (1988). *Writing to learn*. New York: Harper & Row.

Zinsser, W. (1990). *On writing well: An informal guide to writing nonfiction* (4th ed). New York: HarperCollins.

APPENDIX 5.1
Sample Ideas for Entry 3, Activity 1

- Genetic engineering: ethics and societal acceptance of cloning, engineering genes with desirable characteristics, hybrid vegetables, selective breeding. What are the effects on communities? Effect on health care? Insurance?

- Gangs: What is a community's successful response?

- Political cartoons: How do we interpret them and what are their effects on the people who read them?

- Biological warfare: Is its use ever justified?

- Artwork through the ages: students examine any period of history (the Golden Age of Athens, the Middle Ages, the Industrial Revolution, the Great Depression, the 1960s) through the artwork from the period.

- Science through the ages: students examine any period of history through its scientific discoveries and the popular response to these discoveries during that period. Then they apply such insights to today's world: What do modern science discoveries and their popular acceptance portend for us?

- Modern issues/ancient wisdom: Have students research an ancient culture, then determine that culture's stance on modern world issues. For example, how would the Babylonians handle ozone depletion issues? How about censoring lyrics from rap music? Handgun control? Tobacco company litigation? Later, have them portray their ancient culture in a debate over the issues.

APPENDIX 5.2
Sample Analysis of Student Responses: Entry 3, Activity 3

Student A was selected because he is an example of a successful middle-school student in my class. Student A is a conscientious student, with high achievement. He has a reputation for being honest, friendly, and self-disciplined. His work demonstrates strong sensitivity to other people's feelings and an interest in justice. His grades are excellent and he is well regarded by his peers. He is eagerly sought for peer critiques and conferences (seen in the video vignettes). Though he encounters frustrations from time to time, he has made the move from elementary school to middle school successfully without compromising his personality or integrity. The accommodations I have made in order to meet Student A's needs are to accept his work on computer diskette (on which I respond back to Student A), to accept his wishes to read advance-level tradebooks (such as *Fallen Angels*), to embrace his use of narrative structures to demonstrate mastery of content, and to encourage his pursuit of solutions to moral dilemmas expressed in class discussion and literature.

His work over the featured period demonstrates strong abilities. His incorporation of content with narrative voice is particularly strong. For instance, in his story "Lost in the World of the Mayans" Student A researched and incorporated ancient Mayan technology, culture, and village hierarchy in order to create realism in his story about a character's journey into the jungles of the Yucatan Peninsula of Mexico (Student response: [A specific format is required by NBPTS for citing supporting artifacts]). Student A's Learning Log entries exemplify critical thinking and thoughtful response to content reading.

He often points to the irony in historical situations. This is demonstrated in the same passage with his comment that his grandmother used to own a large chunk of a mountain, but as a result of the Depression, she lives in a trailer on a small lot. On the entry dated 12/9, Student A compares a historical fiction character's adventures (Josh's loss of job due to a fire in Irene Hunt's *No Promises in the Wind*) to similar frustration in his own life (handing out fliers for a real estate firm). Student A struggled with moral issues in 12/16/99 entry when he discussed the stealing of food if one was truly desperate. Student A was able to connect with the book's context and emotions in a personal way that gave him meaning.

Student A maintains an organized Learning Log and is able to focus on the content of our lessons (Student response: Interview with Community Leaders). He is able to paraphrase material and present it in a clear fashion (Student response: Gang Issues in Parkdale), and he is able to apply new concepts to different situations (Student response: Socratic Seminar Participation Log).

Student A has areas in which to improve. He occasionally doesn't fully understand directions, as evidenced in the Monitor and Merrimac homework assignment (Student response: Artifact). Also, on some assignments Student A goes beyond the requirements and on others he copies a structure from the presentation, fills in the necessary blanks, and turns in just enough to satisfy the requirements (Student response: Flood Summary). Student A is large for his age, and growing taller by the day. He is often tired, or has a headache, and is learning to balance schoolwork, family, church youth group, a part-time job, and his own interests. This is a year of experimentation for him.

Early Adolescence/ English Language Arts

FAYE WAGONER

Chapter 6 provides the facilitators with:

- An overview of the EA/ELA portfolio entries.
- Assistance in planning activities for candidates in support sessions.
- Information about assessment center activities.
- A list of related resources.

CERTIFICATION CHARACTERISTICS

The Early Adolescence/English Language Arts (EA/ELA) certificate is designed for language arts teachers who teach students ranging in age from 11 to 15. At least 51% of a candidate's students must be in this age range during the time of portfolio preparation for this certificate. Also, the candidate must have completed a minimum of three years in the classroom prior to beginning this certification process. Successful candidates must be able to integrate all strands of language arts: reading, writing, listening, viewing, and language study.

Although candidates are not expected to be experts in any of the following middle-school areas, they should have some knowledge of all of them: learning styles, multiple intelligences (including students with learning disabilities), teacher advisory groups, interdisciplinary lessons/ units, thematic instruction, exploratory programs, block scheduling, conflict resolution, authentic/ alternative assessment, portfolios, use of technology, discipline, and service learning.

STANDARDS

Currently, there are 14 NBPTS standards for the EA/ELA certificate that provide the framework to structure each portfolio entry and to document practice (EA/ELA Portfolio, NBPTS, 1994).

Standard I: Knowledge of Students

Accomplished EA/ELA teachers systematically acquire a sense of their students as individual language learners. Candidates pursue the latest information about early adolescent physical, emotional, social, and intellectual development and what such development implies for educators. The NBPTS is looking for evidence that the candidate knows his or her students and how best to meet their needs.

Candidates also need to demonstrate an understanding of early adolescents as learners in transition. This means incorporating successful middle-school practices wherever possible and understanding why those practices are successful.

Standard II: Curricular Choices

Accomplished EA/ELA teachers set attainable and worthwhile learning goals for students and develop meaningful learning opportunities while extending to students an increasing measure of control over how those goals are pursued. Candidates should document in the entry the variety of texts, media, and technology they present to students. The candidate needs to make clear the appropriateness of selections for early adolescent students in the areas of theme, reading level, interest, and diversity.

Standard III: Engagement

Accomplished EA/ELA teachers elicit a concerted effort in language learning from each of their students. The candidate must document the variety of ways each student is invited to participate and the extent to which each student progresses during the time that the portfolio is being assembled. The videotapes and accompanying commentaries are the best way to show engagement.

Standard IV: Learning Environment

Accomplished EA/ELA teachers create a caring, inclusive, and challenging environment in which students can actively learn. In this area also the candidate must document the variety of settings in which each student is invited to participate. As with the previous standard, the videotapes and accompanying written commentaries are the best way to demonstrate a positive learning environment.

Standard V: Instructional Resources

Accomplished EA/ELA teachers select, adapt, and create curricular resources that support active student exploration of literature and language processes. As with Standard II, candidates should document the variety of texts, media, and technology they present to students. The candidate needs to make clear the appropriateness of chosen resources for early adolescent students in the areas of theme, reading level, interest, and diversity.

Standard VI: Reading

Accomplished EA/ELA teachers engage their students in reading and responding to literature, and in interpreting and thinking deeply about literature and other texts. The candidate needs to demonstrate a focus on developing independent readers; this focus may include providing time to read and providing varied and appropriate reading materials. The candidates might model ways of constructing meaning through journals, small and large group discussions, and interactive media.

Accomplished EA/ELA teachers help students develop criteria for judging the quality of a reading. They provide readings that address complex questions and spark lively discussions. The accomplished teacher realizes that the more meaningful the text—one that speaks to the life of an adolescent—the greater the impact.

Candidates might act as reading coaches for their students. They provide prereading activities to entice participation and new vocabulary to extend student learning and facilitate discussions. They clearly value student ideas and interpretations. Finally, they point to a variety of avenues for students to demonstrate comprehension, interpretation, and appreciation of literature.

Candidates can document these activities through videotapes, lesson plans, samples of reading activities, and student products.

Standard VII: Writing

Accomplished EA/ELA teachers immerse their students in the art of writing. In their portfolios candidates should show the varieties of writing that they encourage students to attempt and the kinds of feedback students receive as they use the writing process. The Analysis of Student Writing Entry of the portfolio is the best opportunity to reflect this standard in depth.

Standard VIII: Discourse

Accomplished EA/ELA teachers foster thoughtful classroom discourse that provides opportunities for students to listen and speak in many ways and for many purposes. The candidate needs to demonstrate in his or her portfolio how students are guided to interpret increasingly demanding texts. The teacher models ways to support interpretations with evidence from the text while valuing differing responses to that same text. Videotaping several of these discussions is valuable for developing the analysis sections of the portfolio. This will also allow the candidate to document student development. The candidate should be able to see him- or herself as a colearner in the discussions.

Standard IX: Language Study

Accomplished EA/ELA teachers strengthen student sensitivity to and proficiency in the appropriate uses of language. This area is really developed through curriculum, reading, writing, and discourse. Seldom is it appropriate to isolate language study. However, candidates should be able to explain in the required written commentaries for each entry exactly how language study is incorporated into each lesson.

Standard X: Integrated Instruction

Accomplished EA/ELA teachers integrate reading, writing, speaking, and listening opportunities in the creation and interpretation of meaningful texts. Candidates need to demonstrate ways they integrate all the strands of language arts so that students make clear connections between the areas being developed as they create and interpret texts.

Standard XI: Assessment

Accomplished EA/ELA teachers use a range of formal and informal assessment methods to monitor student progress, encourage student self-assessment, plan instruction, and report to various audiences. Assessment is an important issue in early adolescent education today, one that warrants careful attention by teaching professionals.

Candidates for NBPTS certification need to demonstrate awareness and use of diverse forms of assessment, including performance, authentic, and alternative assessments. They also need to demonstrate expertise with a variety of scoring structures, including rubrics.

It must be clear to the NBPTS that the candidate provides both formative and summative feedback to early adolescents, and that the feedback is useful. This may require a coaching approach to instruction, too. Candidates need to be able to justify their use of particular assessments for specific assignments. They should document such practices.

Standard XII: Self-Reflection

Accomplished EA/ELA teachers constantly analyze and strengthen the effectiveness and quality of their teaching. This is the power of the process. Thus, it is by looking at how a candidate practices, analyzes mistakes, and models his or her own learning that he or she demonstrates accomplished teaching.

Standard XIII: Professional Community

Accomplished EA/ELA teachers contribute to the improvement of instructional programs, the advancement of knowledge, and the practice of colleagues. This area will be developed in the Documented Accomplishments entries of the portfolio. Encourage your candidates to fully develop a rounded picture of the network of his or her professional relationships. This area lends itself well to keeping a journal that lists and describes committees, conferences, teams, networks, professional development opportunities, and course work.

Standard XIV: Family Outreach

Accomplished EA/ELA teachers work with families to serve the best interests of their children. Candidates need to document the various ways they interact with students' families. Documentation should include samples of formal communications as well as activities used to invite families into the classroom and to encourage a greater partnership between home and school. Keeping copies of newsletters, mailings, assignments, phone logs, invitations to class events, and the like, and describing how they are used to foster family involvement are important in documenting this standard.

HINTS FOR FACILITATORS

✔ Facilitators can help candidates identify the lesson models they tend to use most, and then offer alternative models (e.g., traditional vs. concept attainment models; see Canady & Rettig, 1996).

✔ Candidates may also want to use learning style formats such as the 4MAT system (McCarthy, 1984) or those presented in *Teaching Secondary Students through Their Individual Learning Styles* (Dunn & Dunn, 1993). Such formats encourage candidates to examine which teaching strategies are currently being used, which kinds of students benefit from the various strategies, and what new strategies the candidate him- or herself might wish to try to meet the diverse needs of all his or her students. A useful student text for learning styles is *Learning to Learn* (Frender, 1990).

✔ Facilitators should assist candidates in determining whether the characteristics of the certified field represent the strengths of the candidate.

✔ Candidates must understand and address the standards specific to EA/ELA. The facilitator should discuss and analyze the standards with the candidates.

✔ Remind the candidates that each example must be taken from a different lesson or unit of instruction. Thus candidates will need examples from a wide range of days.

✔ Point out that even unsuccessful examples can have value: even if an example does not turn out as planned, it may prove useful during the analysis stage.

✔ Make sure candidates compare their early drafts to the listed criteria for success (found in "How Will My Response Be Scored?"). Advise candidates to make the necessary comparisons jointly with a colleague; a new perspective often reveals unintended omissions, as well as confirms successful demonstration of the standards.

✔ Point out how important it is for candidates to organize responses in the order indicated in the directions. Following this order ensures that NBPTS assessors can find evidence when they score the response.

✔ Urge candidates to use clear headings and bold type where appropriate, making it clear how all parts of the response fit together. An outline for each entry may help to organize written commentary.

✔ Remind candidates that they must create a context for the assessors to get a clear picture of their classes; while creating this context, they must keep in mind that the assessors do not know the candidate's students.

CERTIFICATION FIELD ORGANIZER

Figure 6.1 provides an overview of the materials related to the EA/ELA portfolio development and assessment center activities. The text that follows elaborates each component.

CREATING EARLY ADOLESCENCE/ENGLISH LANGUAGE ARTS PORTFOLIO ENTRIES

Entry 1: Analysis of Student Response to Literature

Description

This portfolio entry requires the candidate to collect and document three students' responses to literature taught in the classroom. The accompanying written commentary for each student must analyze the teaching practices related to the students' responses. It should demonstrate what the teacher did to set up the response situation. It should discuss the varying ways a student might respond and how the responses show growth in the students over time. The written commentary also allows the candidate to explain the next steps and the ways to change the lesson if teaching it again.

	Portfolio entry	Standard	Hints	Sample activities	Resources
1	Analysis of Student Response to Literature	Refer to Standards I, II, V, VI, XI, XII	–Collect student work early. –Get permissions. –Build a timeline. –Share examples with colleagues.	–Write to standards. –Select student work. –Practice writing. –Analyze student writing.	*Phi Delta Kappan* Magazine. "Ed. Leadership" *The Skillful Teacher* (Saphier & Gower, 1982)
2	Analysis of Student Writing	Refer to Standards I, II, IV, V, VII, VIII, IX, X, XI, XII	–Analyze, don't observe. –Student prior knowledge is important; select range of student abilities. –Know writing theory. –Match to standards.	–Practice analytic writing. –Match responses with standards. –Evaluate examples of teacher feedback on student work.	Journal articles *Seeking Diversity* (Rief, 1992)
3	Instructional Analysis: Small Groups Videotape and written commentary	Refer to Standards: I, II, III, IV, V, VIII, IX, X, XII	–Refer to tips for videotaping. –Plan ahead. –Tape early and tape often. –Show some tapes to the students.	–Analyze tapes early in year. –Take notes/break into observable tasks/look for problems/find impact on student learning/keep a reflective journal.	Tips on videotaping from NBPTS and from this book, Introduction to Part II
4	Instructional Analysis: Whole-Class Discussion Videotape	Refer to Standards I, II, III, IV, V, VIII, IX, X, XII	–Same as previous entry. –Observe candidate role in tape. –Candidate as colearner in discussion.	–Check draft to match to standards.–Conduct Socratic Seminars.	*Circles of Learning* (Johnson, Johnson, & Holubec, 1993) *Positive Classroom Instruction* (Jones, 1996)
5 6	Document Accomplishments I, Professional Community Document Accomplishments II, Outreach to Families and Community	Refer to Standards XII, XIII, XIV	–Don't hesitate to brag; share accomplishments. –Keep a log.	–Set up log of activities. –List resources of potential references. –Keep samples. –Brainstorm types of colleague interactions.	*Enhancing Professional Practice: A Framework for Teaching* (Danielson, 1986)

	Description	Standards	Hints	Sample activities	Resources
Assessment Center	–Background knowledge applied to specific tasks at a testing location. –One day, 6 hours. –Written.	Refer to all standards	–Update professional publications. –Contact colleagues: teachers, principals, university mentors. –Review assessment ctr. orientation booklet; read related materials.	Journal review, group discussion. Jigsaw content and pedagogy. Make up sample questions; do timed writings.	*Voices from the Middle, English Journal, Education Leadership, Phi Delta Kappan,* www.teachnet.org

FIGURE 6.1. Certification Field Organizer: Early Adolescence/English Language Arts (EA/ELA).

The key to success in this entry for the candidate is to select students who will provide complete enough responses to demonstrate progress in their work. The three students should represent a range of abilities so that the candidate can analyze the entire range of his or her practice. Candidates should be able to show the development of the student's interpretation and critical reading abilities.

The three selected students should be those who most clearly show reasoned, in-depth interpretations of literature, given their differing abilities. Candidates need to demonstrate that multiple interpretations by students are valid as long as the student goes back to the text to support his or her opinion. They also want to show their ability to guide students by using appropriate, encouraging feedback. The candidate will select one response from each of the three students. Each response should show a different facet of the literature environment in the classroom.

Standards to Be Addressed

The three student responses as a group must exhibit the following standards:

Standard I: Knowledge of Students
Standard II: Curricular Choices
Standard V: Instructional Resources
Standard VI: Reading
Standard XI: Assessment
Standard XII: Self-Reflection

Hints for Facilitators

Facilitators should advise candidates to consider the following suggestions as they prepare their portfolio responses.

✔ Choose three times as many students to follow as needed for the final written commentary—in this case, the candidate should choose nine. If he or she tries to follow many more in the detail necessary for this project he or she will get bogged down, but fewer might really limit choices later.

✔ Set up folders that contain the writings of each chosen student. The folders should contain a record of why that student was chosen and what goals the candidate has for that student. These goals should include an assessment of the skills the student possessed at the time he or she entered the program.

✔ When collecting student responses, be sure to keep copies of prompts or activities that led to those responses.

✔ Keep copies of feedback given to all the students as well as copies of all follow-up activities.

Activities for Assisting Candidates

ACTIVITY 1: CREATE A TIMELINE

Make a timeline of the activities needed for this entry. Make sure several student response opportunities will fall within the time frame chosen. The candidate will need many student papers in order to have adequate choices when the portfolio is written later.

ACTIVITY 2: BRAINSTORM

Brainstorm classroom activities that candidates already do with literature that reflect Standards I, II, V, VI, XI, and XII. Look for activities that overlap and thus meet several standards. This activity can provide candidates with ideas for lessons that best demonstrate their teaching skills.

ACTIVITY 3: SHARE WRITING

Have candidates bring three to four writings from any student to the group session. In small groups (approx. 4–6) candidates list which standards are demonstrated; analyze the quality of the student responses; look for areas of growth; look for areas that need work; and plan strategies for improvement.

Entry 2: Analysis of Student Writing

Description

This entry requires the candidate to select two students and present three examples of writing from each student. The candidate should choose examples carefully to show the writer's development. If possible, choose both early and later examples to demonstrate how the writer successfully incorporated teacher feedback given on earlier work.

Accomplished EA/ELA teachers immerse their students in the art of writing. By teaching writing as a process, they make it accessible to all students. By serving as a coach, by modeling, and by encouraging writers, they help students focus on audience and purpose. By teaching students to analyze their own writing and to give peer feedback, teachers help students to see themselves as authors and critics. This is an important step in developing a student's voice.

It is critical for candidates to choose students who represent a variety of ability levels. The candidate can best show teaching range if he or she presents a range of students. Often the impact the teacher has is greater at the outset on a student with significant writing problems. But it is also important to show how the candidate can help an already gifted writer to continue to develop.

Remember: these must be *different students* than those followed in the literature exercise. Therefore six additional folders of writing collections will be required. In the written analysis the candidate should always explain how he or she would lead the student to extend his or her learning. These "next steps" are an important part of the reflection.

Standards to Be Addressed

In the entries you choose, the following standards must be addressed:

Standard I: Knowledge of Students
Standard II: Curricular Choice
Standard IV: Learning Environment
Standard V: Instructional Resources
Standard VII: Writing
Standard VIII: Discourse
Standard IX: Language Study
Standard X: Integrated Instruction
Standard XI: Assessment
Standard XII: Self-Reflection

Hints for Facilitators

✔ The best documentation of the teaching of writing is a student portfolio. Remind the candidate that when analyzing the student's writing development, he or she needs to note strengths and weaknesses. But that by itself is not enough. He or she needs to explain what skills the student already possessed before the instruction, what coaching and activities were offered to the student, how those things changed the student's writing, and the next steps that will be attempted.

✔ Often candidates observe but don't analyze. Explain why it is critical that candidates look closely at what worked, ask why, scrutinize what didn't work, ask why, and finally explain changes they propose in their teaching. Analysis puts the sample in context. Remind the candidate that he or she must include all the parts of the required analysis.

✔ Urge the candidate to pay careful attention to the questions in the NBPTS portfolio guide. Make sure the candidate does not get sidetracked, such that he or she only answers parts of them.

✔ The candidate must choose students for this exercise different than those chosen for Entry 1.

✔ As discussed in the Description section, a *range* of student abilities should be represented for both entries.

✔ Teacher feedback on writings should become more sophisticated as the student progresses.

Activities for Assisting Candidates

ACTIVITY 1: LOOKING FOR WRITING PATTERNS

Have candidates bring two or three of their own writings to the joint session to analyze together. The candidates should begin by sharing their writings and looking for patterns. They should identify strengths, weaknesses, and areas that need improvements. By closely examining each other's writings the candidates will improve their abilities to find writing patterns in the work of the students they select as case examples.

ACTIVITY 2: PROVIDING FEEDBACK TO STUDENTS

Candidates should think about the feedback they give to their students. Examine a series of papers written by one student. Ask yourself how does my feedback help this student to make progress? Does my feedback promote real progress or could I do something else to be a more effective teacher?

Appendix 6.1 offers an analysis of student writing; it is included here to show the depth that candidate analysis should reach.

ACTIVITY 3: MAKING CONNECTIONS TO STANDARDS

Have the candidates read the sample student writing analysis in Appendix 6.1. Ask them to identify which standards are exhibited. Then have candidates explain the difference between observation and analysis in the sample.

ACTIVITY 4: GIVING FEEDBACK TO CANDIDATES

The facilitator should regularly offer to review candidate drafts of portfolio written entries. Indeed, one of the most helpful things a facilitator can do is read such entries and identify where each standard is addressed. This kind of feedback not only links candidate writing to the standards, it tells the candidate what is clear and what is murky or missing.

ACTIVITY 5: WRITING AS A TOOL TO COME TO KNOW

Some of the entries required in other certificate fields can prove helpful in the development of the EA/ELA entries. For example, refer to Chapter 5, Entry 1, Activity 2B: Structured Self-Analysis, which focuses on the use of writing as a reflective tool. This entry provides a guide for the practice of EA/ELA candidates as well.

Entry 3: Instructional Analysis—Small Groups

Description

This entry requires the candidate to develop a 20-minute videotape of a small group of students interacting with each other and the teacher. (The NBPTS specifies the number of students required.) The candidate must also write an accompanying commentary analyzing the teaching experiences demonstrated in the videotape. The commentary should explain what led up to the lesson, the makeup of the classroom, how the discussion unfolded, how it met the teacher's expectations, and the next steps the teacher intends to take. It should also include a reflective component that addresses how the teacher will change things next time. **Hint:** When choosing a videotape for analysis, select one that shows students interacting as they normally do.

Standards to Be Addressed

The candidate should address the following standards in the written commentary:

> Standard I: Knowledge of Students
> Standard II: Curricular Choices
> Standard III: Engagement
> Standard IV: Learning Environment
> Standard V: Instructional Resources
> Standard VIII: Discourse
> Standard IX: Language Study
> Standard X: Integrated Instruction
> Standard XII: Self-Reflection

Hints for Facilitators

✔ The candidates will certainly benefit from practical advice on the mechanical process of taping. Please refer to the videotaping hints in the Introduction to Part II of this book and to the "Tips for Videotaping" in the Reference section of the NBPTS's portfolio manual. Everything the candidate (and the facilitator) need to know is clearly covered in this material. Remind the candidates that their success depends on creating quality videotapes.

✔ If the candidate followed the earlier suggestion to tape early and to tape often, this portfolio entry will not be traumatic to him or her.

✔ Remind the candidate to include artifacts (concrete examples) of activities and lessons that preceded the interaction recorded on videotape and that led to the discussion.

✔ Urge the candidates to tape *significant* discussions that show integrated reading, writing, speaking, and listening activities. A tape that shows a caring class environment is not enough; the assessors will be looking for *depth* of discussion.

Activities for Assisting Candidates

ACTIVITY 1: ANALYZING VIDEOTAPES

Ask candidates to create a sample tape or two to bring to a group meeting. Analyze a few of these tapes. Focus discussion on what works well and what doesn't show up in taping. This exercise will help candidates choose the most appropriate lessons to tape. The tapes don't always do what the candidates think they do. Brainstorm ways candidates might most effectively videotape their interaction with students.

ACTIVITY 2: REFLECTING ON PRACTICE

The candidate should videotape a discussion early in the school year, for instance, in October or November. At home he or she should take notes on the videotape, recording each observable task, each standard exhibited, problems, and unexpected occurrences. Then the candidate should bring the tape and his or her notes to group. Facilitator, candidate, and group should share the information and look for areas of agreement and areas missed. Discuss together the impact of the discussion on student learning. Ask the candidate to describe in a reflective journal what best practice would have looked like.

ACTIVITY 3: COLLABORATING ON FEEDBACK

View one of the candidate's tapes in a support session with other candidates. Look for which teaching techniques worked and which ones need improvement. Draw out the candidates' ideas on other ways to handle the situations everyone is observing. Work to help candidates develop objectivity about what they see happening in their classroom.

Entry 4: Instructional Analysis—Whole-Class Discussion

Description

This entry is similar to the previous entry, but it focuses on a whole-class videotaped discussion specific to language arts. The candidate must review the videotape, reflect on it, and analyze the teaching recorded on tape in the written commentary.

Standards to Be Addressed

Entry 4 requires addressing nine standards:

Standard I: Knowledge of Students
Standard II: Curricular Choices
Standard III: Engagement
Standard IV: Learning Environment
Standard V: Instructional Resources
Standard VIII: Discourse

Standard IX: Language Study
Standard X: Integrated Instruction
Standard XII: Self-Reflection

Hints for Facilitators

✔ Encourage each candidate to select a topic for the whole-class discussion that clearly reflects the candidate's knowledge of the EA/ELA curriculum.

✔ Focus on the candidate's role in this discussion. Is active learning happening only for the teacher, or for the teacher and the students together? Is the teacher merely an information source or a true facilitator?

Activities for Assisting Candidates

ACTIVITY 1: ANALYZING GROUP INTERACTION

The candidate should tape a class discussion. Then the candidate should make a chart that notes evidence of some of the following issues: What led up to the discussion? How did it affect some individual students? What vocabulary was learned by students? Were there instances of students expressing individual ideas? Were there instances where the teacher demonstrated valuing of student ideas? The candidate should note which standards were exhibited.

ACTIVITY 2: LINKING TO STANDARDS

The facilitator should read candidate drafts of a written commentary that addresses the questions from the chart developed in Activity 1. Then the facilitator should ask the group to identify the standards that are demonstrated in the writing.

ACTIVITY 3: CONDUCTING A SOCRATIC SEMINAR

The facilitator should share discussion techniques—for example, conducting a Socratic Seminar—that can be used by candidates with their students. (Refer to Chapter 5, Entry 3, Activity 2E for discussion of Socratic Seminar.)

Entries 5 and 6: Documented Accomplishments

Description

Two portfolio entries are common to all certification fields and pertain to work outside the classroom, Entry 5: Collaboration in the Professional Community, and Entry 6: Outreach to Families and Communities.

These entries ask the candidates to demonstrate how they incorporate "a community" into their teaching environment. "Community" is broadly defined and may include families, clients, school neighbors, the school district, and so on. "Community" also includes all professional relationships, such as committees, departments, teams, networks, professional development, and opportunities such as conference or course presentations. Family outreach via phone calls, newsletters, special projects, invitations to class events, and progress reports are included in this entry.

Candidates are asked to provide letters of verification to prove that they actually did each activity. Another adult who can testify that the activity took place is asked to sign and date a letter that substantiates the activity. This person is referred to as a "witness."

Standards to Be Addressed

There are three standards for these entries:

> Standard XII: Self-Reflection
> Standard XIII: Professional Community
> Standard XIV: Family Outreach

Hints for Facilitators

✔ Candidates shouldn't be hesitant to share what they do and how they add to the community of learners in which they live. When candidates develop the written commentary for this entry, they must demonstrate accomplishments that go beyond the classroom. If they don't take the initiative here, no one else will. The NBPTS assessors expect a picture of the candidate's work as a whole. This picture will not be a very clear picture unless it includes descriptions of all the candidate's activities that involve parents, the community at large, and colleagues.

✔ When candidates write about their accomplishments, they must describe the impact their activities had on students, families, the school, colleagues, and the wider community. Self-reflection is evidenced by the candidate's ability to step back and look at his or her activities in a wider context.

✔ Candidates should maintain a log of all their nonclassroom activities throughout the year. This log will help the candidate to find patterns of activities and interfaces that he or she might otherwise miss. Advise candidates to keep log entries up to date; point out that it is very hard to go back later and try to reconstruct this information without an accurate log.

✔ When candidates send communications to students' homes, they should always save copies as evidence of family outreach.

Activities for Assisting Candidates

ACTIVITY 1: DEVELOPING A LOG

For this entry, it is essential to maintain a log of activities for the year. Tell candidates to divide a notebook into sections that match the areas listed in the portfolio instructions (outreach to families, conferences, etc.). Remind them to leave lots of room in each section for potential journal entries.

After they format their logs, the candidates should brainstorm items appropriate for the various sections. Encourage candidates to update their logs weekly and to share new entries with their fellow candidates. All the candidates will benefit from these shared ideas, some of which will inspire them to make their own new log entries.

The log will be a valuable source of evidence when it is time to create this section of the portfolio. Encourage candidates not to be afraid to record seemingly unimportant accomplishments (such as phone calls or feedback on projects); what seems trivial today may prove to be very important later. As always, candidates need to collect more material to work with than will be needed in the final portfolio entry.

ACTIVITY 2: LISTING REFERENCES

Have candidates create a list of potential references. Work with candidates to brainstorm a list of those who may be able to assist the candidate in documenting those community activities, accomplishments, and the like. By beginning the list as soon as the candidate starts the portfolio process, he or she can build support gradually and thereby avoid last-minute panic.

ACTIVITY 3: BRAINSTORMING COMMUNITY CONNECTIONS

In group, brainstorm types of professional relationships and professional development opportunities that show the range of the candidate's work. Look for ways to demonstrate that the candidate, through outreach to families and community, is a member of a learning community and is continuing to grow professionally.

ASSESSMENT CENTER PREPARATION

Description

The assessment center activities provide the candidate with an opportunity to pull together all his or her skills, research, repertoire of strategies, and background knowledge and apply them to specific tasks. At the assessment center the candidate writes four 90-minute essays that require him or her to think "on his (her) feet" and respond to realistic teaching situations. The exercises are tailored to English language arts and students ages 11–15. However, some questions are used to determine how much professional knowledge you have on research and trends in your field. The exercises are chosen from a bank of questions designed by other classroom teachers.

The NBPTS sends an orientation booklet to each candidate that outlines what the candidate may bring to the assessment center and general areas the tasks may cover. The candidate should be very familiar with work across the entire field of EA/ELA.

To prepare, the candidate may want to spend a few days at a college or university library and immerse him- or herself in professional publications such as *Voices from the Middle*, *English Journal*, *Educational Leadership*, *Phi Delta Kappan*, and the like. There are some excellent websites such as ntpi.org (National Teacher Policy Institute) to explore as well. This site has a wonderful, up-to-date library of readings on current educational topics. There are many controversial topics to challenge candidate thinking. If the candidate has considered reasons for his or her views on each topic before coming to the assessment center, he or she will be far ahead of the game.

Standards to Be Addressed

All of the standards for the EA/ELA certification field (I–XIV) provide the candidate with a framework for responding to assessment center activities.

Hints for Facilitators

✔ Candidates need to be aware of current research and trends in the EA/ELA field. The candidate should spend the equivalent of at least a week preparing for the assessment center. Everything learned or thought about in preparation for the assessment center has the potential to increase the candidate's effectiveness as a teacher, even if it is not used directly at the center.

The candidate will expand his or her expertise just because he or she has put so much concentrated thought into his or her craft. Candidates should approach the assessment center confident that they are well read and their terminology is up to date.

✔ Facilitators should read the assessment center orientation booklet for EA/ELA carefully. Assume each thing in it will appear on the test.

✔ Encourage candidates to organize their ideas after they read each question at the assessment center. Assessors can credit ideas more easily if those ideas are organized logically.

✔ Remind candidates that they must stay within the time limits for each essay. They must plan accordingly in order to put down all their ideas. It is important to explain each idea concisely and to give examples when possible.

✔ Recognize that candidates benefit greatly from work with experts in the early adolescent age group and in English language arts content across the age range. Facilitators with connections to universities can give this support by providing expert mentors for candidates or by guiding their professional reading.

✔ Remind the candidates that they really do know a lot about how to teach English to adolescents or they wouldn't be trying to achieve this certificate.

Activities for Assisting Candidates

Activity 1: Hold Collaborative Practice Sessions

Set up practice sessions with candidates, using the NBPTS assessment center material. At least some of the activities candidates will be asked to do are clearly described in the assessment center orientation booklet from the NBPTS. Facilitators and candidates should read it several times, including all of the stimulus material. If an activity is delineated, write it out ahead of time. If not, write sample questions and do some timed writings to get used to the pressure of a timed environment.

Activity 2: Do a Sample Activity with Language Arts Content

Have candidates individually try the sample activity similar to assessment center prompts about proper choice of literature texts described below (and time it). Then share responses and discuss ways to improve the responses.

SAMPLE ACTIVITY

In the assessment center, the candidate will have 90 minutes to analyze the poems listed below, choose three, and explain his or her criteria for selection. First he or she must decide which poems to choose. The facilitator might encourage the candidate to make lists of the advantages and disadvantages of each poem and then decide his or her anthology selections.

The candidate should probably spend about a third of the time analyzing the problem and making decisions. The rest of the time should be spent explaining those decisions. The candidate should be sure to discuss age-appropriateness, theme, interest, and diversity. This is his or her chance to show off an understanding of adolescents.

Finally, the candidate needs to explain exactly why the other two poems were left out. Was there some real objection to them or were they just not as appropriate as the others? Candidates must address every part of each question even if the answer seems obvious to them.

You are an editor for a poetry anthology for seventh grade students. You can only include three of the following five poems in the anthology. Decide which poems you will include and explain your reasons for including or excluding each poem.

"The Road Not Taken," by Robert Frost
"If," by Rudyard Kipling
"Annabelle Lee," by Edgar A. Poe
"The Charge of the Light Brigade," by Alfred Lord Tennyson
"Formula," by Ana Maria Iza
"I'm Nobody, Who are You?" by Emily Dickinson
"Dream Deferred," by Langston Hughes

Activity 3: Connecting to the Standards

Using the responses from Activity 1 above, identify the connections to the standards in the written work the candidates have produced. Reference to the standards will strengthen their response.

Activity 4: Reviewing Current Publications

Have candidates look through publications for the last two years to see what trends are discussed and what topics are current "hot." (The Resources at the end of this chapter provide some suggestions, but candidates may also want to brainstorm their own list in collaboration with facilitators.) Trends and hot topics are likely to show up in the assessment center activities. If the candidate has thought about his or her position on these topics beforehand, then it will be easier to address them during a timed situation.

This is an area of candidate support where university/professional development mentors are very important to increase candidate awareness of current research and new writing in the relevant fields. Candidates could review their ideas with a mentor to clarify them so they can be correctly cited as evidence to back up the candidate's ideas.

RESOURCES

Books

Canady, R., & Rettig, M. (1996). *Teaching in the block: Strategies for engaging active learners*. Princeton, NJ: Eye on Education.

Carnegie Council on Adolescent Development. (1989). *Turning points: Preparing American youth for the 21st century*. Washington, DC: Carnegie Foundation.

Danielson, C. (1986). *Enhancing professional practice: A framework for teaching*. Alexandria, VA: Association for Supervision and Curriculum Development.

Dunn, R., & Dunn, K. (1993). *Teaching secondary students through their individual learning styles: Practical approaches for grades 7–12*. Boston: Allyn & Bacon.

Frender, G. (1990). *Learning to learn*. Nashville, TN: Incentive.

Johnson, D., Johnson, R., & Holubec, E. (1993). *Circles of learning: Cooperation in the classroom*. Edina, MN: Interaction.

Jones, F. (1996). *Positive classroom instruction*. Santa Cruz, CA: Fredric H. Jones & Associates.

McCarthy, B. (1987). *The 4MAT system*. Barrington, IL: Excel.

Rief, L. (1992). *Seeking diversity: Language arts with adolescents*. Portsmouth, NH: Heinemann.

Saphier, J., & Gower, R. (1982). *The skillful teacher: Building your teaching skills*. Carlisle, PA: Research in Better Teaching.

Other useful sources, especially on the writing process, may be found in the Resources at the end of Chapter 5.

Professional Journals

Educational Leadership, Association for Supervision and Curriculum Development

The English Journal, National Council for Teachers of English (high school)

Phi Delta Kappan, Phi Delta Kappa journal

Voices from the Middle, National Council for Teachers of English (grades 6–8)

Websites

www.ncte.org   National Council for Teachers of English

www.nea.org   National Education Association

www.ntpi.org   National Teacher Policy Institute

APPENDIX 6.1
Sample Analysis of Student Writing: Entry 2, Activity 2

The writings of student A were done over a period of four months. They show a range of purposes, audiences, and styles. He is an average writer who has lots to say and is willing to write. He is much more free in his writing when he is role playing than when writing with his own voice. [Documents (artifacts) illustrating student writing may be referenced in the analysis and attached at the end of the portfolio entry.] However, as the class tries more kinds of writing, his confidence increases. His control is expanding.

At the sentence level, A has learned to catch the reader's attention by making a clear and interesting opening statement. When you read the openings of documents II, V, and VI, you can see the purpose of each writing.

At the beginning of the year A did not seem to be able to initiate his writing. He frequently received lowered grades because his work was late. He complained that he could not get his ideas off the ground. In two sessions after school we spent time discussing beginnings and just getting started. He has no trouble continuing after he develops the initial paragraph. We have tried several forms of graphic organizers to plan writings. This technique consistently helped A. He currently uses it frequently for free-choice work. We also explored a "jump into the middle and figure out the beginning later" technique. A is not really comfortable with that, but he will do it if nothing else works.

At the discourse level A's greatest improvements this year are in revision. He says groups help a little. "I like other people's opinions because I can see what they are thinking." However, A says directed revision is much more helpful. This is the technique where I ask direct questions in class and point out things students should look for in their writing. For example, as we revised document III, I asked students to read only their first paragraphs and then put their index finger on the topic sentence. If they could not find it I instructed them to add one. We don't do this as often now, since most students have become more fluent, but A says it makes him slow down and see where he can improve.

A says this year he has taken ownership of his writing. This accounts for the most obvious improvements. His article about his aunt (document III) shows great interest and detail. This interview (in document III) seems to have inspired documents V and VI. You can see that the revisions in the poem go beyond editing. He has searched for the exact words to convey a clear image. Since A knows that he can go back and revise, he finds it easier to get started. He is not paralyzed by the need to have a perfect opening initially.

At the discourse level, A needs to work on parallel sentence structure to convey his ideas more clearly. His unparalleled structure in Document VII is confusing. A is ready to deal with this more complicated writing strategy since his writing has become more complex and detailed. This will be the focus of our next writing conference. He knows that sentences that have to be reread are confusing. He still tries to rush through the editing phase too quickly and thereby misses several errors in each paper.

At the sentence level, A needs to improve his use of apostrophes. They frequently detract from his meaning. In document III he refers to "the dogs point of view." In document VI "in last weeks assignment," "for those who cant," and "less of the persons money" are all examples of missing apostrophes. He grasps the rules, but he reads over the mistakes when he edits. His most effective editing technique is to read the piece aloud to hear mistakes. However, he cannot hear the apostrophes. He needs to address this because it confuses the reader and slows down communication. As A's writing becomes more fluid, small glitches like apostrophes stand out more.

A enjoys writing now. He says he feels more confident and willing to write. He enjoyed the newspaper project and says journalism is a genre he will continue to pursue. I believe that helping a student become a more willing writer is an important step in writing improvement. His recent essay about teaming (document VIII) shows a marked increase in control. His willingness to enter it in a contest shows his increase in confidence.

CHAPTER 7

Adolescence/Young Adulthood/
Mathematics

CONSTANCE MOSAKOWSKY
THOMAS JOHNSON

Chapter 7 provides the facilitators with:

- A description of the AYA/mathematics portfolio entries.
- Information and activities to assist candidates in support sessions.
- An overview of the assessment center activities.
- A list of resources.

CERTIFICATION CHARACTERISTICS

This chapter provides information to assist teachers who are applying for certification in the area of Adolescence/Young Adulthood/Mathematics (AYA/M). What follows is a description of the standards that characterize an accomplished teacher in AYA/M, descriptions of the various entries in the individual teacher candidate's portfolio, and a collection of hints and samples to guide the facilitator in preparing candidates to complete the certification process.

The teacher candidate in this field must have a valid teaching license, at least three years of teaching experience, and be currently teaching at least two mathematics class sections in which the majority of students are in the requisite age range of 14 to 18 or over. For the AYA/M assessment, teachers are expected to provide samples, written or videotaped, of at least four different units of study.

The AYA/M certification includes the following teaching areas: algebra and functions, geometry, calculus, discrete mathematics, and statistics and data analysis.

A candidate has a limited amount of time for preparation of materials; consequently planning must be his or her first activity. Preparation of the portfolio sections must be completed in approximately six months, which will require candidates to devote a minimum of one hour per day to preparation. These candidates must commit themselves to preparing and following a careful schedule.

To support his or her AYA/M candidates the facilitator must read the NBPTS material on certification in general, read and master the material on mathematics certification, and compile lists of reference material and other resources.

This chapter is designed to help facilitators who are using the Collaborative Model of Support presented in this book to support candidate teachers through the NBPTS process. It contains a certification field organizer that provides an overview of the entire assessment, standards, hints for facilitators, activities for use with candidates, and resources.

STANDARDS

The NBPTS has identified 11 standards for AYA/M (AYA/M, NBPTS Portfolio, 1997). Each standard is described below; at the end of each description is a question to provide a focal point for discussion to guide facilitators as they assist candidates in identifying the standards in their own teaching.

Standard I: Commitment to Students and Their Learning

Accomplished mathematics teachers value and acknowledge the individuality and worth of each student, believe that all students can learn and use significant mathematics, and demonstrate their practice. Can the candidate demonstrate how he or she teaches *every* student?

Standard II: Knowledge of Students

Accomplished mathematics teachers use their knowledge of adolescents and of adolescent development and their knowledge about the effects of this development on the learning of mathematics to guide their curricular and instructional decisions. They understand the impacts of home life, cultural background, individual learning differences, student attitudes and aspirations, and community expectations and values on the learning of their students. Can the candidates demonstrate awareness of the student in the context of his or her family, maturity level, and culture, and how is this reflected in his or her teaching?

Standard III: Knowledge of Mathematics

Accomplished mathematics teachers have a broad and deep knowledge of the concepts, principles, techniques ,and reasoning methods of mathematics that they use to set curricular goals and shape their teaching. They understand significant connections among mathematical ideas and the applications of these ideas to problem solving in mathematics, in other disciplines, and in the world outside of school. What evidence exists to demonstrate that the candidate has mastered the subject of mathematics and can apply the broad concepts within the discipline to school-level math?

Standard IV: Knowledge of Teaching Practice

Accomplished mathematics teachers have an extensive base of pedagogical knowledge and use it to make curriculum decisions, to design instructional strategies and assessment plans, and to choose materials and resources for mathematics instruction. How does the candidate demonstrate his or her mastery of the craft of teaching?

Standard V: The Art of Teaching

Accomplished mathematics teachers stimulate and facilitate student learning by using a wide range of formats and procedures and by assuming a variety of roles to guide students' learning of mathematics. What are the best approaches to student math learning and how does the candidate demonstrate their use?

Standard VI: Learning Environment

Accomplished mathematics teachers help students learn mathematics by creating environments in which students assume responsibility for learning, show willingness to take intellectual risks, develop confidence and self-esteem, and value mathematics. How does the candidate create an environment that facilitates discourse among students (individually and in groups), where all students can experience the power of math learning?

Standard VII: Reasoning and Thinking Mathematically

Accomplished mathematics teachers develop students' abilities to reason and think mathematically; to investigate and explore patterns; to discover structures and relationships; to formulate and solve problems; and to justify and communicate their conclusions. In what ways does the candidate help students develop math reasoning?

Standard VIII: Assessment

Accomplished mathematics teachers employ a range of formal and informal assessment methods to evaluate student learning in light of well-defined goals. They use the results to inform the teaching process and provide opportunities for students to reflect on the strengths and weaknesses of their individual performances. How does the candidate assess students for different purposes and in different ways?

Standard IX: Reflection and Growth

Accomplished mathematics teachers regularly reflect on what they teach and how they teach. They keep abreast of changes in mathematics and in mathematical pedagogy, continually seeking to improve their knowledge and practice. How does the candidate demonstrate continual professional growth?

Standard X: Families and Communities

Accomplished mathematics teachers support the involvement of families in their children's education, help the community understand the role of mathematics and mathematics instruction in today's world, and, to the extent possible, involve the community in support of instruction. How does the candidate communicate with the people in the school community?

Standard XI: Contributing to the Professional Community

Accomplished mathematics teachers collaborate with peers and other education professionals to strengthen their school's programs, advance knowledge, and contribute to improving practice within the field. In what ways does the candidate demonstrate work with other teachers and with teaching organizations?

GENERAL HINTS FOR FACILITATORS

✔ The facilitator should establish a support group consisting of him- or herself, the candidates, and resource people who can help the candidates with various parts of their portfolios. The ideal group of resource people could include a mathematician, a math educator (especially one familiar with the National Council of Teachers of Mathematics [NCTM] standards), a videotaping specialist, an NBCT, or a writing specialist.

✔ After establishing the support group, the facilitator should set up a regular schedule for meetings (preferably weekly). The meetings must allow enough time to review portfolio entries, review assessments, discuss accomplishments, and answer candidate questions about various portfolio activities.

✔ The facilitator should either know the content required for the AYA/M certification or know someone in mathematics or in math education who can work with the candidates to evaluate and/or discuss the candidates' mathematical thinking and enhance their content knowledge.

✔ Facilitators should encourage candidates to become familiar with the standards in mathematics at the local, state, and national levels. (See Resources at the end of this chapter.)

✔ Make sure that the candidates are aware of the hints, carry out suggestions, and stick to their timelines.

✔ Encourage the candidates to reread all the analysis prompts for each type of activity in the entry before planning the activity. This will provide the necessary structure for responding to the prompts in each analysis.

CERTIFICATION FIELD ORGANIZER

Figure 7.1 offers a concise overview of the portfolio entries required for AYA/M certification, the associated standards, facilitator hints, sample activities, and useful resources. All of the material is explained in detail in the remainder of this chapter.

CREATING ADOLESCENCE/YOUNG ADULTHOOD/ MATHEMATICS PORTFOLIO ENTRIES

Entry 1: Analysis of Student Work—Applications

Description

This entry asks the candidate to demonstrate the teaching process by selecting the responses of three students (all from the same class) to an assignment or prompt. The candidate must answer 10 specific questions about the student responses. The candidate analyzes the assignment given to his or her students and explains its particular purpose and its place in the curriculum. In com-

	Portfolio entry	Standard	Hints	Sample activities	Resources
1	Analysis of Student Work: Application	Refer to Standards I, II, III, IV, V, VI, VII	−Read NBPTS material before working with candidates. −Plan. −Select students. −See Questions/Descriptions.	−Graphing circles. −Defining prompts. −Practicing responses. −Analyzing student work. −Chapter 5 exercise.	−Review prompts in AYA/M portfolio.
2	Analysis of Student Work: Assessment	Refer to Standards I, II, III, IV, VII, VIII	−Overprepare. −Math and pedagogical ideas to help in math. −Collect several assessments.	−Discussion of requirements. −Brainstorm assessment. −Assessment analysis. −Sharing student responses. −Feedback to students.	−Review 10 prompts in AYA/M portfolio. −NCTM standards series.
3	Instructional Analysis: Whole-Class Videotape	Refer to Standards I, II, III, IV, V, VI, VII	−Videotaping hints can be generalized for both large and small groups.	−Brainstorm topics. −Collaborative video analysis. −Using NBCT tapes. −Writing to sample prompts.	−Videotaping hints. −Video expert/NBCT.
4	Instructional Analysis: Small-Group Videotape	Refer to Standards I, II, III, IV, V, VI, VII, IX	−Build confidence in teacher and students by taping often. −Collaborate with peers, students, and facilitators	−Response to prompts. −Sharing classroom activities. −Videotape analysis. −NBCT input.	See Videotaping hints in the Introduction to Part II.
5	Document Accomplishments I, Families and Communities Document Accomplishment II, Professional Community	Refer to Standards IX, X, XI	−Start early. −Record often. −Keep a box for artifacts.	−Evaluation of entries. −Data collection.	

	Description	Standards	Hints	Sample activities	Resources
Assessment center	Demonstrate your knowledge of both pedagogy and content in 4 of 5 domains	Refer to all Standards	−Know resources. −Read. −Come prepared.	−Read. −Practice assessment center prompts. −Update skills. −NBCT input.	Assessment center activities from NBPTS.

FIGURE 7.1. Certification Field Organizer: Adolescence/Young Adult/Mathematics (AYA/M).

plimentary fashion, the candidate analyzes the student responses to demonstrate both his or her knowledge of the students and his or her ability to evaluate the mathematical learning and reasoning that took place in the exercise.

The candidate's principle evidence of student progress is the written work that each student provides in response to the prompt (a specific assignment, worksheet, test, or other assessment) from the teacher. How does the student respond to the prompt? What does the student submit in response? How is the response analyzed by the teacher? What feedback is the student given concerning his or her work? How does the student response inform the teacher's decisions about future lessons? These issues are addressed in Entry 1 and again in Entry 2; both involve written work from students.

Standards to Be Addressed

All of the standards listed below must be considered in the responses to this entry:

Standard I: Commitment to Students and Their Learning
Standard II: Knowledge of Students
Standard III: Knowledge of Mathematics
Standard IV: Knowledge of Teaching Practice
Standard V: The Art of Teaching
Standard VI: Learning Environment
Standard VII: Reasoning and Thinking Mathematically

Hints for Facilitators

✔ Obviously, candidates should be encouraged to choose an activity that lends itself to the type of analysis that will be required. This means that the activity should encourage mathematical thinking, require the students to make and test conjectures and come to conclusions, and fit logically into the curriculum.

✔ Facilitators should trumpet the value of redundancy. Advise the candidates to collect several activities from different classes. Moreover, they should begin with more than three students for each exercise.

✔ They should choose students with different ability levels whose work represents a wide range of results.

✔ Candidates will need to document their reasons for choosing these particular students. They will also need to include personal data on each student, such as the student's past performance or any learning issues. Beginning now, they should use all of the resources available to them to get to know their students.

✔ The students to be highlighted in this entry should not be selected until the candidates have gathered enough material to make valid choices.

✔ Encourage candidates to keep detailed, ongoing records of each exercise or activity. This data will help them to analyze the entire activity, including the feedback they give concerning each submitted work.

✔ Make sure that candidates collect release forms for all of the students at the start of the year.

Activities for Assisting Candidates

ACTIVITY 1: DEFINING NBPTS PROMPTS

Encourage candidates to read over the prompts for Entry 1 included in the portfolio. Discuss the meanings of the prompts and how they might apply to specific classroom circumstances and curriculum.

ACTIVITY 2: PRACTICING RESPONSES

To encourage candidates to practice responding to the prompts for this entry, the facilitator can use the sample from a math lesson on graphing circles found in Appendix 7.1 at the end of this chapter. He or she can also ask candidates to bring in samples from their own classrooms. Lead discussion by using the set of questions found below (on Activity 5). The sampling can be used in two ways: as an introduction to a discussion about ways to meet the criteria for this entry and/or to assist the candidate in looking for connections to the standards for the entry.

ACTIVITY 3: LINKING LESSON AND UNIT GOALS

The facilitator can ask candidates to share a lesson they use in their classes, providing their rationale for using this (these) particular assignment(s) or prompt(s) to enhance their overall learning goals for the lesson, for the unit, and for the year.

ACTIVITY 4: SHARING EXAMPLES

Have candidates bring in several samples of activities from their classes that meet the criteria and the standards for this entry. Have them present their samples to the group and discuss the characteristics of an effective analysis. Candidates could also present an analysis of a lesson, and the facilitator or the group could respond by assessing the effectiveness of the candidate's analysis.

ACTIVITY 5: ANALYZING STUDENT WORK

Have candidates choose a sample of one student's work and analyze that sample with these questions in mind:

> What were your goals for the lesson?
> Did the student learn what you expected him or her to learn?
> What evidence do you have?
> What evidence in the student's work shows that mathematical reasoning and thinking took place?
> What will be the next step in your instruction?

Divide the support group into small groups to discuss the candidates' responses.

ACTIVITY 6: MAKING CONNECTIONS TO MATHEMATICS

This entry expects candidates to think about ways that mathematics is integrated with other disciplines. To encourage candidates to think about this integration, facilitators could ask candidates to write about their math integration for one week. They can do a structured self analysis with such questions as:

> What math is being learned?
> What misconceptions are still evident?
> What worked?
> What didn't work?
> What will I do differently tomorrow as a result of what happened today?
> Whose needs are not being met?
> How does this lesson fit into the larger picture?
> Are the students building meaning for themselves or am I doing it for them?
> Is this material useful to their lives?
> How intellectually rigorous is this material?
> How can I tell the students are learning?
> Were the students prepared for this lesson?
> Why or why not?

The facilitator and candidates could review the discussion of Entry 2, for the EA/G portfolio, in Chapter 5. This entry requires generalists to "explore connections to mathematics" and provides good advice for this entry too.

ACTIVITY 7: REVIEWING LITERATURE

See Chapter 5, Entry 2, Activity 2.

Entry 2: Analysis of Student Work—Assessment

Description

This entry asks the candidate to select three student responses to an assessment or test as an illustration of the teaching process. In a written commentary, the candidate is asked to respond to 10 specific prompts. The assessment/test must be analyzed both for its place in the curriculum and for how it assesses learning of a specific unit or topic. Similarly, the student responses are analyzed to demonstrate both the teacher's knowledge of the student and his or her ability to analyze the mathematical learning and reasoning that are illustrated in the test. Additionally, this entry provides an opportunity for the candidate to describe how assessment affects instructional decisions.

Standards to Be Addressed

Entry 2 involves the following standards:

> Standard I: Commitment to Students and Their Learning
> Standard II: Knowledge of Students
> Standard III: Knowledge of Mathematics
> Standard IV: Knowledge of Teaching Practice
> Standard VII: Reasoning and Thinking Mathematically
> Standard VIII: Assessment

Hints for Facilitators

✔ Encourage candidates to read and understand the 10 prompts found in the AYA/M portfolio before they begin to prepare their assessment.

✔ Encourage candidates to plan assessments based on the type of prompts to which they will respond. Since they will be asked to explain their students' mathematical reasoning and how they reached conclusions, candidates should include questions in the assessment that call for reasoning and reaching conclusions.

✔ Remind candidates that they must plan and document their assessment carefully. They will be asked to describe what each question has to do with the mathematics curriculum and why it was asked. They will also be asked to explain how the learning goals for the unit are reflected in the questions that they asked.

✔ Arrange for candidates to meet together to practice responding to the requirements of this AYA/M entry.

✔ Encourage candidates to keep records of the oral and/or written feedback that they provide to students. They will be asked what feedback method they used and why they used it for each test/assessment and for each student whose work they submit.

✔ Encourage candidates to collect several assessments. They should use more than one class and more than three students. Such redundancy now will allow the candidates to choose those responses that best exemplify their practices to include in the final entry later.

✔ Remind candidates that they need to choose students with a variety of ability levels. Thus they must have student backgrounds in mind when they choose students to include in preparing the analysis. They must also consider the students' past work, how they respond to the teaching situations, and what they do during class.

✔ The most important resources in preparing for this entry are the NCTM publications and mathematics texts.

Activities for Assisting Candidates

ACTIVITY 1: DISCUSSING REQUIREMENTS

The facilitators and the candidates should jointly read over the prompts to which the latter must respond for Entry 2. Discuss the meanings of the prompts and how they might apply to specific assessments or tests. Discuss the ways in which the assessments developed by the group also address the standards required of this entry.

ACTIVITY 2: BRAINSTORMING ASSESSMENTS

Reminding them to keep the portfolio prompts in mind, have candidates brainstorm a list of different types of assessments and then discuss the value to student learning of using varying types of assessments for their analysis. The NCTM book on assessment (cited in Resources at the end of this chapter) includes some valuable examples.

ACTIVITY 3: ANALYZING ASSESSMENTS

Ask candidates to bring to group a copy of an assessment they use at the end of a unit. Have candidates answer the following questions: How does this assessment fit into the skill goals for the unit? How does the assessment reflect the knowledge/learning goals for the unit?

Have candidates share their responses. Discuss alternative assessments that might achieve similar goals.

ACTIVITY 4: SHARING STUDENT RESPONSES TO AN ASSESSMENT

Have each candidate bring in a sample of one student's test/assessment and then analyze that assessment in group with these questions in mind:

Why did you select this student?
What were your learning goals for the unit being assessed?
Did the student learn what you expected?
What evidence in the student's work shows that mathematical reasoning and thinking took place?
What will be the next steps in your instruction?

Relate all responses to the standards for this entry.

ACTIVITY 5: EVALUATING CANDIDATE FEEDBACK TO STUDENTS

Suggest that candidates bring in samples of student responses to an assessment that also contain their own feedback to those student responses. Discuss the role of the feedback to (1) address the teacher's goals for student learning, and (2) provide information to inform future instruction.

Entry 3: Instructional Analysis—Whole Group

Description

This section is intended to illustrate teaching (via videotape) as the candidate engages the whole class during a 20-minute segment. The whole class is expected to interact with the teacher as they consider together some mathematical concept, principle, technique, or reasoning method. The teacher's commentary consists of responses to nine prompts that probe the teacher's planning for the year, planning for the class, evaluation of the class presentation, and what was learned by the teacher from the exercise.

The goal of the videotaped exercises is to provide the assessor with the best possible evidence of classroom practice: the teacher in action in concert with the students. The candidate must be aware that the assessor wants to see the final product: how the class actually progresses, how the students engage the material, how growth takes place. The 20-minute videotape and the accompanying written analysis is intended to illustrate the candidate's familiarity with and commitment to students, knowledge of mathematics, ability to create a positive classroom environment, and his or her skill in promoting mathematical thinking and reasoning between and among students.

Standards to Be Addressed

Entry 3 involves the following standards:

Standard I: Commitment to Students and Their Learning
Standard II: Knowledge of Students
Standard III: Knowledge of Mathematics
Standard IV: Knowledge of Teaching Practice
Standard V: The Art of Teaching
Standard VI: Learning Environment

Standard VII: Reasoning and Thinking Mathematically
Standard VII: Assessment
Standard IX: Reflection and Growth

Hints for Facilitators

General hints on videotaping are found in the Introduction to Part II; see Videotaping: Technical Aspects and Videotaping: Analysis. All these hints are applicable to both the whole-class (Entry 3) and small-group (Entry 4) portfolio exercises.

✔ Encourage each candidate to enlist someone to assist with videotaping. Ideally, this person would have videotaping expertise. Good resource people would include a library/media specialist or a colleague with videotaping expertise.

✔ Encourage candidates to read all the advice related to videotaping that is included in this book and in the NBPTS portfolio.

✔ Urge candidates to get permission slips signed by all their students during the first few days of the school year. Remind them to first make sure they are all legible, and then to store them in a safe place. These slips must be submitted with the candidate tapes.

✔ You cannot repeat this mantra often enough: "Start videotaping early. Videotape often! Videotape all classes!"

✔ Urge candidates to experiment to find the best locations in their classrooms for the students and their desks, the camera and the camera operator, and themselves. Remind them to make sure the faces of their students are showing. Remind them to pay close attention to the lighting (both natural and artificial). Urge them to experiment with the recording of the sound (*wearing a body mike is very helpful*).

✔ The candidates should be reminded that they are to look for a segment for each submission (20 minutes, unedited) that flows from one activity to another.

Activities for Assisting Candidates

ACTIVITY 1: BRAINSTORMING TOPICS

Encourage the candidates to brainstorm topics that will take and hold the interest of the whole class. Have them create scenarios for different ability levels and different subjects with the topics previously listed during the brainstorming. Remind candidates that it is best to show different activities during each of the taped segments. Appendix 5.1 contains several activities to encourage thinking "outside the box." In particular, Activity 3 focuses on making connections with other contents and might provide additional examples to encourage discussion with candidates.

ACTIVITY 2: COLLABORATING ON VIDEOTAPE ANALYSIS

Have candidates bring in videotapes to share with the group. As a group, analyze and critique the videos. Focus on questions such as:

What standards are being addressed?
Is the tape of good enough quality, in terms of both audio and video, for the assessor?
Does the tape lend itself to answering the prompts in the portfolio?

ACTIVITY 3: USING NBCT VIDEOTAPES

If possible, have an NBCT share his or her tapes with the group. This will give candidates a much better idea of what is expected of them. The tapes do not have to be in the math certification field. Regardless of the content of the tapes, candidates should be encouraged to analyze the tapes by answering such questions as:

What is the context of this segment?
What is the content represented?
How does the structure of the class, the lesson, and the student response illustrate the designated standards?

ACTIVITY 4: PRACTICING WRITTEN COMMENTARY

Candidates should practice writing responses to sample prompts. Using a discussion format, have them critique each other's work. Have them brainstorm alternative responses. In this activity, facilitator feedback is very important to keep candidates focused on *analysis* of student learning in mathematics.

Entry 4: Instructional Analysis—Small Groups

Description

This entry is intended to illustrate the candidate teaching as he or she interacts with small groups of students in the class during a 20-minute videotaped segment. The videotape should show the candidate working with two or more groups as they engage in a mathematical exercise. The written commentary consists of responses to nine prompts that probe the candidate's planning for the year, planning for the class, evaluation of what the students accomplished during the class and during the tape, and what the candidate learned from the exercise.

Standards to Be Addressed

The following standards are applicable to Entry 4:

Standard I: Commitment to Students and Their Learning
Standard II: Knowledge of Students
Standard III: Knowledge of Mathematics
Standard IV: Knowledge of Teaching Practice
Standard V: The Art of Teaching
Standard VI: Learning Environment
Standard VII: Reasoning and Thinking Mathematically
Standard IX: Reflection and Growth

Hint for Facilitators

✔ This entry requires a videotape. The hints for this entry are the same as those for Entry 3 and are delineated in that entry.

Activities for Assisting Candidates

ACTIVITY 1: RESPONDING TO PROMPTS

Appendix 7.2 at the end of the chapter offers an example of a response to prompts similar to ones that may be contained in the portfolio. The facilitators can help the candidates to critique the sample response, then brainstorm other possible responses and the relationship of each response to the standards.

ACTIVITY 2: SHARING CLASSROOM ACTIVITIES

Have candidates bring in classroom activities to present to the support group. Have them practice responses. Evaluate these responses as they relate to the required prompts and the required standards. Brainstorm alternative activities that might more effectively demonstrate the standards.

ACTIVITY 3: ANALYZING VIDEOTAPES

Have candidates bring in videotapes they have made to share with the group. Analyze and critique the videos, keeping the following questions in mind:

> What standards are being met?
> Is the candidate interacting with small groups as defined in the portfolio?
> Is the quality of the tape good?
> What improvements can be made?

The candidates should practice descriptive, analytic, and reflective responses.

ACTIVITY 4: NBCT INPUT

If possible, invite an NBCT to a group meeting to share his or her videotapes with the group.

Entries 5 and 6: Documented Accomplishments

Description

Documented Accomplishments consists of two parts: Entry 5, documenting active collaboration in the professional community, and Entry 6, documenting active involvement with families and communities. The candidate must address activities that demonstrate both. Each activity must be verified either by a document or by an individual familiar with the activity.

The activity for Entry 5, Professional Community, is slightly different. In this activity the candidate's work over the past five years must be documented and submitted. It is important for candidates to obtain documentation for activities from prior years as soon as possible. Examples might include: work with the school district or state on a curriculum planning committee, work in connection with a local or regional teachers' convention, presentation of a paper before any audience of teachers, work with practice teachers or interns, work with a local college of education, or work as a mentor in the candidate's own school. The activity involving Entry 6, Families and Communities, is intended to reflect the teacher's connection to the parents, the community of the school, and the community of the neighborhood.

Standards to Be Addressed

The following two standards apply to Entries 5 and 6:

> Standard X: Families and Communities
> Standard XI: Contributing to the Professional Community

Hints for Facilitators

✔ Encourage the candidates to read all of the materials for Entries 5 and 6 *before* they begin work on these entries.

✔ Candidates should be encouraged to use their vacation time during the summer before they actually begin work on the portfolio to reflect on their accomplishments outside the classroom. It is difficult to remember everything you have done for the past five years while you are teaching.

✔ Advise candidates to choose carefully among their various outside activities. The candidate may choose as many activities as he or she wishes, but must fully document each activity. Such documentation can be time-consuming.

✔ Encourage candidates to try to contact as many people as possible who can verify their activities/accomplishments. Warn them that there is a limit on how many items each person can verify.

✔ Remind candidates that while professional activities are documented for the past five years, community activities must be limited to those that take place during the school year in which the portfolio is prepared.

✔ Encourage candidates to set up a file system to keep their write-ups and verifications organized. As soon as possible, they should begin to structure the collection, categorizing and storing relevant data to document this portion of the portfolio.

✔ Urge the candidates to begin a "Parental Contact Log" immediately! It should provide space to include *all* contacts: phone calls, informal notes, school visits, incidental contacts, and the like. They should keep it up to date on at least a weekly basis. It might include, but is not limited to: careful records of extracurricular activities; communications with parents, such as report cards, notes, midadvisory or midquarter reports, and other types of progress reports; and any assignments that require parent involvement.

✔ Suggest that candidates:
  • Extend invitations to parents at the beginning of the year to visit and speak to classes.
  • Keep records of contacts with social workers, counselors, administrators, special education teachers, and the like, that concern individual students.
  • Keep records of any tutoring of students, whether arranged or done by the candidate.
  • Keep records of any school committees on which the candidate serves that also involve parents. Records should include meeting dates and accomplishments
  • Make a list of all professional organizations to which he or she belongs.

✔ Ask candidates the following questions:
  • Did you participate in any community activity related to the accreditation of your school? Be sure to provide particulars.
  • Did you supervise standardized testing or provide interim and/or final examinations for your department?

- Did you integrate any course content across another content area?
- During the past five years, have you taken any courses or attended any workshops related to mathematics or the teaching of mathematics?

Activities to Assist Candidates

ACTIVITY 1: EVALUATION OF ENTRIES

Appendix 7.3 contains examples for Entry 5. Evaluate these examples by comparing them to the standards. Brainstorm alternative ways to address the standards. Remember that assessors will need to find clear connections and evidence between the candidate's work and the NBPTS standards for these entries. Next have candidates brainstorm way to address Entry 6.

ACTIVITY 2: DATA COLLECTION

Have candidates create journals (brainstorm categories of information) and document files (brainstorm lists of possible topics). As they collect data, time should be set aside in group meetings to share the information collected with other candidates in the group.

ASSESSMENT CENTER PREPARATION

Description

The assessment center activity is unlike any prior experience that the candidate will have had in the NBPTS process, since both pedagogy and subject area mastery are evaluated in a timed assessment. The candidate must be prepared to demonstrate mastery of the material in four of five domains: algebra and functions, geometry, calculus, discrete mathematics, and statistics and data analysis. The responses inquire both about the content and about the presentation of the material. The content prompts will be ordinary test questions designed to explore how familiar the candidate is with that particular domain. The presentation prompts will probe the candidate's ability to present the material and then evaluate the student responses. The candidate will spend one day at the assessment center (The NBPTS uses Sylvan Learning Centers for the assessment) and will respond to prompts in 90-minute blocks. Candidates will receive information about some of the prompts prior to going to the assessment center.

Standards to Be Addressed

All of the standards are addressed during the assessment center activities.

Hints for Facilitators

✔ The facilitator can assist candidates by making them aware of refresher courses or tutorial opportunities. Not every candidate will have up-to-date familiarity with four different domains in mathematics. Teachers who work with one grade level may only be familiar with one of the domains and will obviously need assistance in three others. The facilitator should work to connect the candidates with university faculty in mathematics education, knowledgeable colleagues, and other candidates who have mastery of other domains to help them update their knowledge and skills. The facilitator can match candidates in the support group who can be helpful to one another—for example, a candidate strong in algebra can be matched with a candidate who needs help in this domain.

✔ The facilitator should urge candidates to become familiar with the NCTM standards as well as all of the NBPTS standards (see Resources at end of this chapter.) Remind them that most of the questions will test their knowledge based on current thinking in mathematics education.

✔ Share the Resources at the end of this chapter with candidates; it lists resources on up-to-date mathematics instructional thinking.

✔ Urge candidates to conduct an in-depth review of any domain—statistics, algebra, discrete math—if they have not taught this subject area for a long time. They should get their hands on a well-written current textbook and go through it.

✔ Urge candidates to take advantage of any refresher courses provided in their school system or local community.

✔ Remind candidates that they are not facing a standard content test. Pedagogy—how one introduces or illustrates a topic—will be a big part of the assessment.

✔ Since graphing calculators are permitted, urge candidates to practice with their calculators beforehand.

✔ Facilitators should advise candidates to bring all the supplies—drawing tools, erasers, pencils, extra batteries, and the like—that the NBPTS allows to the assessment center.

✔ Advise candidates to use all the practice materials supplied by the NBPTS.

Activities for Assisting Candidates

Activity 1: Practice Assessment Center Activities

Have the candidates complete the activities provided in the "Assessment Center Guide" from NBPTS. Have them keep a record of the time it takes them to finish the activities. Use at least one meeting to share and discuss their answers to these activities.

Activity 2: Update Skills and Knowledge

Facilitators could arrange tutoring sessions and/or collaborative group sessions for candidates who request a "refresher" in any of the tested areas.

Activity 3: NBCT Input

If possible, arrange to have an NBCT in mathematics talk to the group about the assessment center process.

RESOURCES

Professional Journals

National Council of Teachers of Mathematics, 1906 Association Drive, Reston, VA 22091-1593. Phone: 1-703-620-9840; fax: 1-703-476-297; website: www.nctm.org. Provides access to important journals as well as conferences at the national, state, and local levels.

The Mathematics Teacher. Journal for teachers of secondary mathematics (grade 8 through two-year and teacher education colleges).
Mathematics Teaching in the Middle School. Journal for teachers of mathematics, grades 6–8.
Teaching Children Mathematics. Journal for teachers of mathematics (grades K–6).
NCTM Yearbooks. These yearly publications provide valuable information on developments in the field, activities for classes, and teaching strategies as well as professional articles.

The National Council of Teachers of Mathematics (NCTM) Standards series listed below is also available on-line at www.nctm.org:

National Council of Teachers of Mathematics. (1989). *Curriculum and evaluation standards for school mathematics*. Reston, VA: Author.
National Council of Teachers of Mathematics. (1991). *Professional standards for teaching mathematics*. Reston, VA: Author.
National Council of Teachers of Mathematics. (1995). *Assessment standards for school mathematics*. Reston, VA: Author.
National Council of Teachers of Mathematics. (1996). *Mathematics: An introduction to the NCTM standards*. Reston, VA: Author.
National Council of Teachers of Mathematics. (1998). *Standards 2000 Project: The principles and standards for school mathematics* [On-line resource]. Available April 1, 2000 at: www.nctm.org/standards2000/.

Miscellaneous

State and local Mathematics Teacher Organizations, branches of the NCTM, also have journals and resource lists.

Association for Supervision and Curriculum Development (ASCD) publishes a journal, *Educational Leadership*, with research articles.

Textbooks sent to your school for evaluation or textbooks available at NCTM conventions provide sample lessons and valuable resource material.

APPENDIX 7.1
Sample Classroom Activity: Entry 1, Activity 2

2A. Linking Lessons to Student Learning

To begin a discussion, facilitators could ask candidates to address questions such as "What might be the learning goals (lesson objectives) for the lesson to which the attached sample (Figure 7.2) responds?" "What connections did you expect students to make?"

Sample Response for Discussion

Lesson goals and learning objectives: Students will be able to:

1. Solve an equation of a circle for y.
2. Practice using a graphing calculator to graph circles using both the $y =$ and the circle draw features.
3. Discover how the value of r affects the graph of $x^2 + y^2 = r^2$.
4. Write the equation of a circle given its graph.
5. Review prior knowledge: a circle with center at (h, k) and radius r has equation $(x - h)^2 + (y - k)^2 = r^2$.
6. Demonstrate mastery by making your own designs.

These objectives allow students to discover that the center of a circle with equation $x^2 + y^2 = r^2$ is at the origin; that the value of r enlarges or reduces the circle; that when using the "circle draw" function on the TI-82, (h, k, r) are the values entered; that they can write the equation of any circle knowing the values for h, k, and r.

2B. Fitting Lessons into the Instructional Sequence

Using the same lesson sample (Graphing Circles; Figure 7.2), or lessons brought by the candidates, the facilitator can ask candidates to briefly describe where this assignment might be effectively placed into their instructional sequence for the unit. Candidates could brainstorm additions to the sample(s) that would provide a rationale for this placement.

Sample Response for Discussion

The class has just begin a unit on circles. Equations of circles are briefly covered in the first lesson of the unit. The day before the students worked on this assignment, I taught them how to solve an equation of a circle for y so it could be entered into a graphing calculator. I also showed them how to use the circle to draw feature and had them practice graphing circles using both methods.

Name _____

1. Use your graphing calculator to graph each of the equations below. Adjust the screen on the calculator by pressing Zoom Square. You will first have to solve each equation for y in terms of x. Graph both of the resulting functions in y_1 and y_2. (Each will be one-half of the circle.) Then complete the chart. The first entry has been completed for you.

Equation	y in terms of x	r	sketch	x and y intercepts
$x^2 + y^2 = 25$	$y = \pm\sqrt{25 - x^2}$	5		$(\pm 5, 0), (0, \pm 5)$
$x^2 + y^2 = 4$				
$x^2 + y^2 = 100$				
$x^2 + y^2 = 0$				
$x^2 + y^2 = 8.1$				

2. Use the results of Exercise 1 to answer the following questions.
    a. Which graphs cross the x-axis? _____
        y-axis? _____
    b. Does changing the value of r affect the location of the center? _____
        If so, how? _____
    c. If r increases, what happens to the circle? _____
    d. If r decreases, what happens to the circle? _____
    e. Why must $r > 0$? _____

3. Make up an equation whose graph is a circle between the graphs of the equations $x^2 + y^2 = 4$ and $x^2 + y^2 = 5$. _____

4. Write an equation whose graph is a circle with center at $(0,0)$ and has intercepts $(\pm 8, 0)$ and $(0, \pm 8)$.

    _____

    _____

(cont.)

FIGURE 7.2. Graphing calculator activity.

5. Examine the design below and find a set of equations that form a possible solution. Then use your graphing calculator to test your equations. When you have found a correct set, list the equations you used. There are many possible solutions.

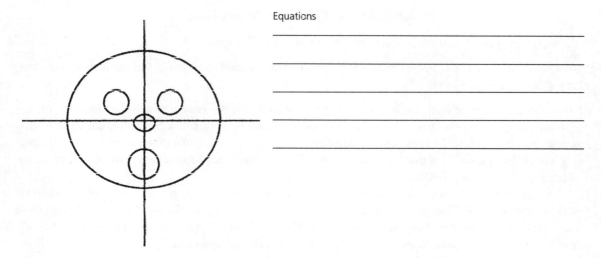

Equations

_____

_____

_____

_____

_____

FIGURE 7.2 *(cont.)*

APPENDIX 7.2
Sample Responses: Entry 4, Activity 1

Response A: Geometry Worksheet

All responses represent student work with material found in Figure 7.3.

Question: What particular instructional challenges do the selected students in the small groups chosen for this videotape present?

I try to make sure that each student in the group understands the concepts and the solutions to the problems they are working on. Often weaker students tend to want to let the better students in the group do all the work while they observe. However, this is not as much of a problem now, in the spring, as it was at the beginning of the year. The students have learned that I expect everyone in the group to be able to explain the solutions to me.

As the year progresses, many of the groups need little or no guidance from me. They get right to work. Others need a "jump start" to get going. There are a few groups who want to split up the problems, with each group member doing just a part of the assignment. I have discouraged this practice all year, but it is hard to change some behaviors. In this class, the students usually stay "on task," but there have been exceptions to this practice. I circulate around the room, observing each group to make sure they are working together, and give help when needed.

For the most part, the students in this class get along with each other. However, there is one young man that no one (except his closest friends) wants to work with. The reason they do not want to work with him is because he is one of the underachievers mentioned earlier, content to let others do the work for him while he distracts everyone sitting around him. On the tape, he is the one who said he was not listening. I have paired him with one of his friends, an excellent student. The friend usually manages to keep him on track most of the time.

There are the usual personality conflicts that exist in any group of ninth-grade students, but these cause no problems because the students were able to choose their groups, as explained in the answer to the previous question.

Response B: Video Analysis

Question: Which interactions on the video clip show that a student[s] is learning to reason and think mathematically? Please explain as specifically as possible. A candidate might respond as follows:

At the beginning of the tape, the first two groups, each made up of three girls, were thinking and reasoning mathematically to arrive at the answer to the area problem (#7, Figure 7.3). At 3 min. 16 sec. into the tape, the two boys working together were not sure of their answers. By my trying to make them actually think about what they had to do, they were able to reason through the rest of the problem. At 4 min. 30 sec., the group of three boys (with the backpack on the table) were helping each other understand how the solution was reached. At 8 min. 20 sec., we see the two boys discover the pattern needed to solve the problem they were on. At about 12 min. 50 sec., the two girls who were having trouble getting started were able to reason through the rest of the problem as soon as I helped them to see what they had to do first. At 15 min. 56 sec., the boy who was having trouble seeing that the quarter ($.25) problem (#2, Figure 7.3) would work the same with pennies made the connection that circles are similar and that their radii are proportional. At 16 min. 18 sec., we see a boy explaining the pattern to his female partner. The girl who was asking me how to do the problem at 18 min. 20 sec. was looking for an easier way to find the answer to number 10. She did not think "trial and error" was a very efficient method.

1. The pyramid of cans shown at the right has four layers with a total of 20 cans. How many cans are there in a similar pyramid of 10 layers? _____

2. A quarter remains still while a second quarter is rolled around it without slipping. How many times does the second coin rotate around its own axis? _____

3. Find the next term in the sequence 0, 2, 42, 170, 682. Describe the pattern

   _____

4. Find the next number in the sequence 3, 6, 11, 18, 27. Describe the pattern

   _____

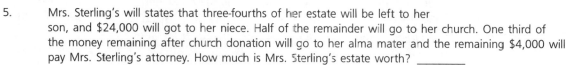

5. Mrs. Sterling's will states that three-fourths of her estate will be left to her son, and $24,000 will got to her niece. Half of the remainder will go to her church. One third of the money remaining after church donation will go to her alma mater and the remaining $4,000 will pay Mrs. Sterling's attorney. How much is Mrs. Sterling's estate worth? _____

6. Complete the multiplication problem at the right. Each digit 1–9 is used exactly once.

$$
\begin{array}{r}
2\_\_ \\
\times \quad 1\_ \\
\hline
5\_\_\_
\end{array}
$$

7. If the length of a side of a square is s, then the area of the square is $A = s \times s$, or s^2. In the diagram below, the area of square H is 64 square units and the area of square F is 49 units. Find the areas of the other seven squares

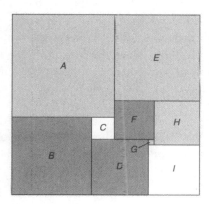

A = _____   D = _____   I = _____
B = _____   E = _____
C = _____   G = _____

FIGURE 7.3. Example of exercises students were working on in a videotape used for sample responses to Entry 4, Activity 1. From *Merrill Geometry: Applications and Connections* (1993) by G. F. Burrill, J. J. Cummins, T. D. Kanold, and L. E. Yunkers (pp. 400–401). Woodland Hills, CA: Glencoe/McGraw-Hill. Copyright 1993 by Glencoe/McGraw-Hill. Reprinted by permission.

APPENDIX 7.3
Examples for Entry 5, Activity 1

Note: Examples refer to professional activities carried out over the last five years that involve the local school district or another local education organizations.

Example A

My school is exclusively for ninth-graders, and has been in existence for about 18 years. During our first year, the math courses offered were ESL math, Pre-Algebra, Algebra I, Geometry, and Algebra II. Because the state has mandated that all students learn algebra skills, and because the Pre-Algebra classes were overcrowded and not successful for students, the math teachers at my school decided to develop and implement a new two-year course designed for students with a history of math difficulties. We wanted to limit the class size and set up a course that encouraged student success.

I was one of the three math teachers who developed the curriculum for this course called Algebra I, Part I. We decided on the content to be included, set up a timeline, worked on alternative ways of presenting the content, developed supplementary materials, and developed projects that could be used to enhance classroom learning. A detailed curriculum guide, our final product, was presented to the teachers teaching the course. We have continued to revise, enhance, and update this curriculum over the two years the course has been taught.

Example B

For the past four years, I have worked with the members of the Mathematics Department (grades 7–12) and the administration of a neighboring school to implement the *Standards* adopted by the National Council of Teachers of Mathematics (NCTM). The previous curriculum did not provide consistency from year to year and there was no agreement on prerequisites or outcomes. Emphasis on Standard VI (Learning Environment) and Standard VII (Mathematical Reasoning) were missing from the earlier curriculum. I encouraged department members to join the NCTM. Together we reshaped the curriculum. We standardized the overall program, making sure to provide instruction for all ability and interest levels. The changes we made reflected both the changing needs of the scholastic and occupational communities and the changing technology that is becoming available. We brought the curriculum into alignment with what students had previously been taught in grades K–6 and what they would be expected to know in college.

PART THREE

Post-Candidacy

Our inability to answer every question about teacher effectiveness right now shouldn't make us reluctant to use the devices we do have to begun to lure the best in, screen others out, and intensively develop the rest.
—HAYCOCK (1998)

Insights from National Board Certified Teachers

BARBARA COLE BROWNE

Valuing teachers' voluntary, ongoing changes in practice is one way of empowering them in the process of educational improvement.
—KADEL-TARAS (1998, p. 151)

Chapter 8 provides facilitators with information on:

- Candidate recognition.
- A candidate reflective group activity.
- Impact of NBPTS on teaching practice.

The previous chapters covered the overall process for certification from the NBPTS, the Pre-Candidacy phase associated with the introductory seminar, and the Candidacy phase consisting of portfolio preparation and assessment center activities. This chapter discusses the Post-Candidacy phase, including activities and opportunities for teachers after their completion of the assessment process, and suggests ways to recognize National Board Certified Teachers (NBCTs). NBCTs are at the center of this chapter: they provide us with answers to questions regarding the importance of the NBPTS certification process, its impact on their own practices, and the experiences that emerge as they engage in expanded roles as teacher leaders.

CANDIDATE RECOGNITION

After NBPTS candidates complete the assessment process, the facilitator should organize an event to celebrate the accomplishments of *all* the candidates. This celebration will validate the work of all the candidates and recognize their professional commitment to go beyond the usual professional development opportunities to learn and reflect about their own teaching practices.

All candidates, including those who do not achieve certification, should be recognized for their efforts related to NBPTS certification. A reception for candidates is an ideal social event to honor their commitment to their profession. The facilitator, who by now knows all the candidates well, should take the lead in coordinating and organizing the event. Remember that public announcement of candidates' names can be made *only* after each candidate has given permission for his or her name to be announced. The NBPTS is very clear that participation in the assessment process is a voluntary, confidential experience; therefore, only candidates themselves determine when and where their names will become public.

REFLECTIVE GROUP ACTIVITY

The reflective group activity is designed to bring the candidates together for an open discussion of issues regarding the NBPTS process.

The reflective group sessions should bring together the NBPTS candidates after they have completed their assessment center activities but before they have been notified about whether they have achieved certification. This timing ensures that the candidates focus on the *positive* experiences of the NBPTS assessment process while it is not yet connected to certification or noncertification. The reflective groups can be small; for example, they can be limited only to those candidates who were in the same certification field support groups established during the Candidacy phase of the process. The group need only meet once, typically in the early fall, as candidates are usually notified about certification by the NBPTS in November.

The facilitator can use the following questions to guide group discussion. They center on how a candidate's teaching has changed by taking part in the assessment activities. Candidates supported by our Collaborative Model of Support provided input into the following questions.

1. **What did I learn from the NBPTS assessment process and the support I received?** Discussion related to this question provides input about how the process changed candidates' approach to their teaching. Many candidates revealed that by this stage in the NBPTS assessment process they have become more reflective about their teaching. Teachers report that they keep the NBPTS standards in mind during their daily teaching and that these standards provide a framework to evaluate their daily teaching practices. Candidates also report that the support network encourages ongoing collaboration among the candidates and expands their thinking about practices in their certification field.

2. **How did I positively change my teaching?** The impact of the NBPTS process is important only if it changes teaching positively and if those changes have an impact on student achievement. As of today, research on impact is limited. However, anecdotal evidence from teachers who have participated in the support sessions indicates that after completing the NPBTS assessment process, they feel better prepared to monitor their student's growth and progress and to evaluate individual student progress throughout the year. In addition, they report that the experience provided them with the opportunity to expand their leadership roles in the educational community.

3. **How can the support group established during the Candidacy phase continue to support those who do not achieve certification?** Not all teachers achieve NBPTS certification the

first time they try. Teachers who choose to continue the process by "banking" their better scores and revising selected components of their portfolio will benefit from ongoing support. For this reason, we promote the cyclical nature of the Collaborative Model of Support. As candidates become NBCTs, they can provide practical support to both continuing and new candidates. NBCTs can become actively involved in leadership roles, for example, by facilitating the introductory seminar and support group sessions. Since NBCTs have valuable resources and information to share, they can be an important source of ongoing support.

Question 3 asks teachers to reflect on support that might be helpful to them during the "banking" experience. Candidates usually develop a very close collegial network during candidacy that can be helpful and supportive to those who do not achieve certification. By establishing the parameters of support for those who don't achieve prior to actual notification about certification, colleagues can obtain insights into what support would be beneficial and can help to maintain the collegial relationships developed during candidacy.

THE IMPACT OF NBPTS ON THE PROFESSION

The NBPTS process promotes and challenges teachers not only to be "accomplished teachers," but also to reach out to the community and promote learning in a broader sense. This has certainly been the case with the teachers who received support in our Collaborative Model of Support.

NBCTs provide valuable insights about "accomplished teaching." Most importantly, they helped to address the following questions: Why is it important for teachers to seek NBPTS certification? What is the impact of the NBPTS certification process on teachers and teacher leadership? What is its impact on students and learning? The answers to these questions can be used by facilitators to encourage teachers to seek NBPTS certification and to encourage others to support these teachers. The responses provided below were derived from informal discussions during the reflective group activity, through telephone interviews with candidates, and from unsolicited written testimonies from candidates who received support from the Collaborative Model of Support.

1. **Why is it important for teachers to seek NBPTS Certification?** The testimony of teachers who actually experienced the NBPTS assessment process offers compelling evidence of why it is important for teachers to seek NBPTS certification. As NBCTs indicated, the assessment process recognizes teaching accomplishments, provides professional recognition, and promotes collaboration.

Teaching can be an isolating experience. Accomplished teachers often do not receive the positive recognition and rewards they deserve. The NBPTS assessment process provides an avenue to recognize teaching accomplishments. The first group of NBCTs were invited to the White House by President Clinton to receive national recognition of their achievement of NBPTS certification. Carol Sultzman, an Early Adolescence/English Language Arts Certified Teacher, revealed that she was particularly pleased by this experience because it focused on a group of teachers who were all being recognized for documenting their professional teaching accomplishments. At the White House event, NBPTS certification provided the reason for the president to recognize teachers who had worked very hard, who had documented their teaching, and who were being recognized together as truly exemplary practitioners.

The NBPTS process offers opportunities for collaboration among teacher colleagues. The introductory seminar and support group activities both provide ways for teachers to engage in professional dialogue and receive and share information with others, thereby connecting the expertise of practicing professionals. One teacher revealed that one of the most rewarding elements of the certification process was the professional, collaborative relationship that developed with her partner teacher. The building of professional relationships and the strong community of accomplished educators who challenge one another to strive for excellence is very rewarding indeed. Many NBCTs report that such collaboration continues after they have achieved NBPTS certification.

2. **What is the impact of the NBPTS process on teachers and teacher leadership?** The NBPTS process promotes teachers as change agents/role models, decision makers/advocates, reflective practitioners, teacher educators, and leaders. Teachers who have achieved NBPTS certification through the Collaborative Model of Support now enjoy enhanced professional status among their peers and in the educational community.

NBPTS certification extends the roles of teachers and at the same time allows teachers to remain in the classroom. As Rick Wormeli, an Early Adolescence/Generalist NBCT states, "The [NBPTS] certification process brings dignity and professionalism to a job some communities do not believe to be worthy of such a designation. It provides a way to move up in teaching without leaving the classroom, an elusive goal thus far."

NBCTs can have an impact on changing and strengthening the teaching profession by mentoring new candidates and being role models for other teachers. For example, many NBCTs support new candidates as they seek NBPTS certification. This support provides candidates with input from an accomplished teacher/mentor, and provides the NBCT with an opportunity to continue to learn and grow from sharing with peers in the same field. As Governor James Hunt from North Carolina said in a speech to a group of NBPTS, "You are all part of a beautiful tapestry. The strength of the fabric depends on the strength of each thread. Each of you is a thread" (Hunt, 1997). NBCTs can be part of that "tapestry" as they support other teachers to better understand and reflect on their practice.

NBCTs are decision makers and advocates. They can have an impact on what happens in their own systems as well as in their statewide systems. NBCTs have been invited to speak to school boards regarding the impact of the NBPTS process on their teaching; have been invited to help develop standards for students at the state level; and today are working on local, state, and national issues related to the NBPTS. These efforts include promoting the value of NBPTS certification and encouraging the development of incentives such as the reimbursement of the fee to promote the availability of NBPTS certification to all teachers.

Developing strong networks of support helps to extend the professional development aspect of the NBPTS assessment process and encourages continued reflection. NBCTs report that they continually reflect on their practice and integrate the NBPTS standards into their teaching on a daily basis. One NBCT teaches in kindergarten through grade six as a reading specialist. She writes lessons daily, shares them with other teachers, leads professional development workshops, and collaborates with other colleagues to solve questions about her practice. All of these actions lead to more effective teaching. Another benefit of the assessment process that NBCTs report is that they look forward to reflecting on their practice by collaborating with other teachers. When teachers feel comfortable sharing their ideas and collaborating to improve upon their daily teaching they can enhance their own teaching, enhance their colleagues' teaching, and thus benefit the children in their classes.

Many NBCTs also become teacher educators in both pre-service and professional development programs. They are an untapped resource that should be a primary component of any teacher development program. NBCTs have been invited to lecture in university courses in their fields of certification. The real-life experiences they bring to the university classes blend theory with practice from the perspective of a truly accomplished teacher. The NBPTS standards and NBCTs are increasingly providing a link between university programs and actual practice in the field (Browne, Auton, & Futrell, 1998).

As internship supervisors, NBCTs are using the NBPTS standards to direct their work with student interns. The standards provide a framework to promote critical thinking in the interns and help interns clarify and articulate reasons for using certain approaches with children. As Marlene Henriques, an Early Childhood/Generalist NBCT, states, "I can use the National Board standards to tell my student teachers why I use certain approaches in the classroom so they can better understand the relationship between theory and practice and apply those principles to their own teaching someday."

Teacher leadership opportunities have expanded as more and more teachers have achieved NBPTS certification. The leadership roles of the NBCTs supported by our Collaborative Model are many and varied. Their experiences mirror the leadership opportunities of many NBCTs around the country. They serve as presenters at workshops at the local, cross-district, state, and national levels; they present and speak at regional and national conferences; they serve on boards representing teachers and teacher groups; they write articles and books on their areas of content, pedagogy, and education in general; and they serve as representatives on teacher leadership groups at the local, state, and national levels, where they work to improve the quality of education for all students and to promote national educational reform.

The collaborative thinking promoted during the NBPTS assessment process extends beyond that experience. NBCTs share their experiences, work with others, and extend their work and expertise to the larger educational community, thus potentially improving education for all students.

3. **What is the impact of the NBPTS process on students and learning?** The National Commission on Teaching and America's Future (1996, p. 7) declared: "What teachers know and can do makes the crucial difference in what children learn. Student learning in this country will improve only when we focus our efforts on improving teaching."

A focus on what teachers need to know and be able to do in order to be successful with their students is primary to the NBPTS assessment process, as well as to our development of the Collaborative Model of Support. NBCTs continually demonstrate the impact that the NBPTS assessment process and its standards can have on their own practice and subsequently on their students' learning and on the community at large. In the following section NBCTs share what the process has meant to them and their teaching and how it has had an impact on student learning. The voices of these teachers are representative of what many NBCTs tell us about how the NBPTS assessment process has positively impacted their students' learning.

The NBPTS standards have a positive impact on teaching practice and encourage reflective practice.

Nancy Areglado, an Early Childhood/Generalist NBCT, discusses how the standards have improved her teaching and fostered reflective practice:

"The accomplished teacher knowingly interweaves the standards throughout all parts of a lesson. The standards have been an all-encompassing lever for me to invigorate my teaching by making sure that I incorporate them in lesson planning, execution, and reflecting. They have become internalized and are a part of my teaching.

"The children I teach grow and learn because when I strive to make myself a better teacher, they profit from that experience. I now know that practicing reflection frees teachers to be active learners, researchers, and innovators of the education profession. The standards allow me to take the risk to evaluate myself honestly and provide the opportunity to grow and change . . . and when we have room to grow we can really begin to teach and cultivate learning in every child. Each day I now stop and reflect continually on my craft. I constantly ask myself questions: Am I meeting my students' needs and empowering them as learners? Am I well-enough prepared? Is there a resource available that I should read to improve upon the lesson and better meet students' needs? Am I helping other teachers I work with to learn and grow? Am I meeting the goals that I set for myself to be a better teacher for all children?"

Reflecting on teaching and integrating the NBPTS standards into teaching is a way of life for most NBCTs. They are committed to better serving children by continually growing and learning as professionals.

The NBPTS assessment process broadens a teacher's understanding of children and helps create meaningful curriculum and strategies.

Carol Sultzman, an Early Adolescence/English Language Arts NBCT, discusses how the NBPTS process has had an impact on her teaching and on her students:

> "Because of the NBPTS certification process, I am better able to create a more competent and defensible instructional program based on my understanding of the total process involved in the education of a child. I have experienced, firsthand, the process moving from simply 'thinking about what I do' to reflective practice.
>
> "In completing the portfolio, I was required to analyze every aspect of my teaching. From classroom management to curricular decisions to methods of assessment, I was required for the first time to seriously consider the quality and validity of my teaching against national standards. I discovered my own insecurities and strengths. I was able to uncover the connective skills and knowledge children need as they advance from kindergarten to high school and become interactive learners with one another, which is sometimes forgotten.
>
> "Going through the NBPTS process increases one's awareness of the need for sound pedagogical practices and, more importantly, school-based decision making by knowledgeable and competent professionals. The analytical teacher demands thoughtful reasoning in instructional decisions that support student success. The NBPTS assessment process fosters positive dialogue, and those who participate in this dialogue bring back to the classroom, and thus to the children they teach, the lessons learned from self-analysis."

The NBPTS process is meaningful and challenges a teacher's practice.

Carol Horn, an Early Adolescence/Generalist NBCT, shares her thoughts about the NBPTS process:

> "The NBPTS process is the most meaningful evaluation I have ever experienced. It challenged me to think and reflect on the best teaching practices that I could use in my classroom with my students on a daily basis. I felt that my students greatly benefited because of the reflection and the opportunities it gave me to collaborate with other teachers. I constantly revised what I was doing and I continue to do that as a NBCT. The process reinforced a lot of the positive ideas I had read about good teaching practice. I realized how important it was to develop a community of learners and have my students engaged in the learning process.

"I also realized the importance of integrating all the different subject areas, and I spent a lot more time thinking of ways to integrate language arts and science and social studies. I just kept looking for connections in various subject areas and looking for ways that I could relate what I was teaching to something that would be meaningful in the lives of my students."

The NBPTS process focuses on the uniqueness of each student and encourages family involvement.

Lisa Holm, an Early Childhood/Generalist NBCT, states:

"The NBPTS assessment process demonstrated my commitment to students and their learning by providing a wide range of activities for them that incorporated both diverse learning styles and multiple intelligences. I was also encouraged to involve families in the learning experiences that provided opportunities to link classroom experiences with interacting with families. By incorporating family traditions and experiences, I was able to demonstrate to families what was important to the children as learners and the families were a part of the learning process."

Many NBCTs teachers used the NBPTS process in unique ways to improve their practice.

One NBCT modeled the concept of preparing a portfolio to document one's work and writing about it in his classroom. He put portions of his portfolio for the NBPTS up on the wall to share with his students. They watched and saw what he did and how he responded to inquiries about his teaching practices. The students were asked to look at their work, reflect, and change it based on feedback from their peers and their teacher. In this manner they were learning to become reflective learners, a skill they can integrate into their learning as they continue to grow and learn throughout life.

Another NBCT produced multiple videos of her classroom as she prepared her portfolio. She used these videos to help families understand what was happening in the classroom and how their children were interacting in the kindergarten community. She sent the videos home to her families, an exercise that brought the classroom and learning into the home.

The teachers who shared their reflections and experiences in this chapter provide evidence of the benefits of the NBPTS process on teaching, on student learning, on teacher leadership, and on changing practices to exemplify excellence in teaching. While evidence of the impact of the NBPTS process on teaching and children is just emerging, these teachers demonstrate that positive changes are happening in their work with students.

SUMMARY

The potential for improving education is endless with committed teachers who care about children, who care about their profession, and who are willing to take risks to meet national standards and become "accomplished" teachers and leaders in the field. Our Collaborative Model of Support brings teachers and teacher educators together to support teacher candidates preparing for NBPTS certification. The development of the Collaborative Model of Support put teachers in the center of changing practice and led to leadership opportunities for NBCTs (Browne, Auton, & Futrell, 1998).

REFERENCES

Browne, B., Auton, S., & Futrell, M. (1998, April). *Creating partnerships to improve quality teaching: Reflections from a partnership.* Washington, DC: National Council for the Accreditation of Teacher Education (NCATE).

Hunt, J. (1997, fall). Speech presented at National Board Teacher Reception, the White House, Washington, DC.

Kadel-Taras, S. (1998). Teacher centered for teacher change. In D. J. McIntyre & D. M. Byrd (Eds.), *Strategies for career-long teacher education* (pp. 140–153). Thousand Oaks, CA: Corwin Press.

National Commission on Teaching and America's Future. (1996). *What matters most: Teaching for America's future, summary report.* New York: Author.

The NBPTS and Implications for Education Reform

KATHLEEN ANDERSON STEEVES

Chapter 9 provides facilitators with:

- A summary of the collaborative process of NBPTS assessment.
- A discussion of implications of the NBPTS certification process for higher education and professional development.

What teachers do in classrooms and with their school communities matters in terms of effective school change. Scholars and researchers concerned with education issues have repeatedly identified teachers as the key to effective student learning or—as has been obvious recently—have blamed teachers for a lack of student success. The Collaborative Model of Support described in this book is effective in preparing experienced teachers to successfully document their practice and achieve NBPTS certification—recognition that they are highly accomplished teachers. That result and the close link between effective teachers and better student learning suggests that utilizing the NBPTS's core propositions and the collaborative process described in this book has merit in the teaching profession's broader efforts to enhance learning for all students. Most importantly, recognized, accomplished teachers are at the center of this change (see Rigden, 1996; Rose, 1999).

THE NATIONAL BOARD FOR PROFESSIONAL TEACHING STANDARDS PROCESS AND EDUCATION CHANGE

Our work with teachers seeking NBPTS certification through our Collaborative Model of Support has raised our awareness of how this process can lead to change in the education system by its focus in four areas:

- Encouraging collaboration and partnerships among the education communities.
- Improving the quality of teacher preparation programs.
- Providing a structure to guide professional development programs across the continuum of a teacher's career.
- Promoting teacher leadership in building the profession and creating long-term educational change.

Encouraging Collaboration and Partnerships

In working with teachers during the development of our Collaborative Model of Support, we highlighted the importance of collaboration and the essential role it plays in training, assessing, and encouraging effective teachers. The prime measure of a highly effective teacher is knowledge of content and pedagogy. This is identified as essential to real student learning in the NBPTS (1998) core propositions, as well as in other standards documents, such as that of the Interstate New Teacher Assessment and Support Consortium (INTASC; 1992), which sets standards for new teachers. All these measures indicate that the link between schools, colleges and universities, and the content standards groups is very significant. The closer and more consistent the linkages, the more current, diverse, and effective the knowledge base of the teacher, resulting in even stronger outcomes for students.

Colleges and universities that prepare teachers may contribute in several significant ways to the preparation of and ongoing increases in knowledge for teachers. As a first step, those institutions must ensure that the students they admit meet the content standards in their proposed teaching field. Once the U.S. population recognizes that teachers entering P–12 schools have a strong content base that they continue to develop while teaching, then teachers will be regarded as professionals and experts in their fields.

Second, a recognition of the importance of strengthened content knowledge should prompt colleges and universities to promote linkages between teacher educators, their students, and content specialists in arts and sciences, engineering, and other fields. Unfortunately, for a variety of reasons, this seldom occurs in U.S. higher education. For example, one study (Steeves, 1998) in the area of history indicated that in most higher education institutions, the work of training history teachers is done *outside* history departments. If content knowledge is important, and we believe it is, then the data highlighted in *What Matters Most: Teaching and America's Future* (National Commission Teaching and America's Future, 1996, p. 15) indicating that almost 50% of mathematics teachers and almost one-third of social studies teachers did not major in their main teaching field should further encourage this collaboration. Moreover, the content knowledge required within the NBPTS assessment process draws heavily on the standards of the specific disciplines, such as mathematics, science, English/language arts, and social studies-history. Here, working relationships with discipline-based associations (e.g., National Council of Teachers of Mathematics [NCTM], National Council for Teachers of English [NCTE], etc.) are also important and bring additional nonuniversity organizations into the collaboration.

Important partners also exist within the education community, broadly defined. The NBPTS notes that effective teachers are connected in meaningful ways to school and professional learning communities. Within the business world the notion of workers as parts of communities in which each individual and the organization as a whole benefit by working and learning together is not new. Corporations have increasingly promoted the "learning organization" over the past decade. This concept has been strongly touted by respected writers on management such as Peter Senge (1990) and Chris Argyris (1992). Regarding the education community, Lambert, Collay, Dietz, Kent, and Richert (1996) describe learning communities in schools as "organizations in which members recognize their interdependence and view the community as a whole" (p. 65). They stress the importance of this type of collaboration as an effective change strategy. Whether teachers are seeking knowledge, training, improved schools, or enhanced student learning, their goals are shared by many outside the teaching profession. While business and education may define their "community" differently, both recognize the value of sharing ideas and expertise to advance the whole organization.

Various groups are beginning to recognize their direct connection to the community of effective teachers—and thus the need for their investment in successful schools. As the NBPTS began its effort to positively affect teacher practice, a number of other groups coordinated their efforts with the NBPTS itself or around its core propositions. Among those are INTASC and the National Council on Accreditation in Teacher Education (NCATE). INTASC provides 10 standards that delineate the assessment criteria for beginning teachers (National Commission on Teaching and America's Future, 1996, p. 73), while NCATE has begun to link its assessment of teacher preparation programs to NBPTS's core propositions and INTASC's standards. Additionally, the work of the various disciplinary organizations (e.g., in mathematics, English language arts, history) is forming the basis for state learning standards for students and are thus becoming part of the assessment process for teachers as they participate in the NBPTS or INTASC assessments. This larger educational community of standards organizations is coalescing to provide a measure of teacher excellence across the continuum of a teacher's career. The community includes university teacher preparation programs, school professional staff development programs, and state and national content standards organizations. As Rigden (1996, p. 64) notes, "Reform in teacher education must include closer collaboration between universities and schools, authentic teacher training and staff development, and stronger support mechanisms for new teachers."

As the education community joins together to improve teachers and teaching, it is vital for school administrators to become involved in the process. Toward that end, a committee within the Council of Chief State School Officers (1996) is currently developing induction standards for principals that place student learning at their core. Each of the standards begins with the phrase "A school administrator is an educational leader who promotes the success of all students by . . . " (p. 8). It is intended that preparation and evaluation of school administrators be guided by these standards.

Like-minded organizations—ranging from educational to governmental to business or community groups—are seeking to collaborate. Such collaboration should be encouraged. It will only be effective, however, if all aspects of the broad teacher role in the education system can be highlighted. To change student learning effectively, collaborative efforts must continue throughout a teacher's career. Everyone, from those who work to prepare teachers to those who provide professional development, from those who work with schools as community members invested in the student graduates, to those who develop the content knowledge and oversee professional and content standards, must become involved. Our experiences at the local level have reinforced our belief in the value of this integrated, collaborative approach to school change that is part of the broader collaboration that is building a new professional community for educators across the nation.

Improving the Quality of Teacher Preparation

Support for practicing teachers seeking NBPTS certification informed our central university mission of preservice education. The NBPTS core propositions, though developed to assess practicing teachers, provide a strong, well-documented set of principles to guide teacher preparation programs. It was obvious from our work with NBPTS candidates that the information provided in the support sessions was integral to the competencies of our teacher preparation programs.

The review process being conducted at George Washington University for all of our teacher preparation programs continues to be guided by the core propositions of the NBPTS and their close cousins, the INTASC standards. For example, the NBPTS and INTASC standards agree that reflection is essential to good teaching. This process should be introduced at the beginning of teacher training and should be practiced throughout a teacher's career. We have reviewed all of the courses in the master's programs in secondary and in early childhood education (a review of elementary education and special education are underway). We will identify where, within each course, the standards (e.g., reflection or knowledge in content and pedagogy) are being addressed.

In early childhood special education, for example, the faculty have aligned their program competencies (derived from recommendations regarding quality teacher preparation from national organizations such as the NAEYC, the ATE, and the CEC/DEC) with the NBPTS's standards. Faculty in the program have restructured program components and revised or developed new program contents in course work and assignments.

Our goal is to ensure that students who complete the master's program in teacher preparation are aware of and able to practice all of these principles as constant tools in their teaching. Again, the standards set by the NBPTS for experienced teachers served as an effective guide for program review. As students prepare their portfolios for final review, acquisition of this knowledge has given confidence to our graduate teachers entering schools for the first time.

Professional Development across a Teacher's Career

The NBPTS core propositions have also been integrated into or guide the development of standards that apply across the careers of teachers. In practice, those principles illustrate the integrated nature of teacher professionalism and student learning. They provide a framework to develop a core of effective, knowledgeable education professionals, whose practice is based in the classroom, but whose network reaches into the community. This process involves not only those universities and colleges that are involved in initial licensure, but also those that can guide the professional development plans of a school system.

One of the NBPTS core principles can serve as an example. NBPTS teacher candidates in all content areas must demonstrate that they know their subjects and how to relate those subjects to students. The development of this skill and knowledge illustrates the continuous nature of the process over the entire career of a teacher. This continuum should be at the heart of decisions when prospective teachers enter undergraduate or graduate programs in teacher preparation. Colleges and universities with quality pre-service programs should consistently evaluate and then adjust their admission processes and their programs, based upon the success of their graduates as active teachers. For example, admissions and training that do not address the current issues of culturally responsive pedagogy (Langsdon-Billings, 1994; Delpit, 1995) may disadvantage the teacher of diverse students in multilevel schools. This same issue may be at the core of courses in child or adolescent development, in specific methods or content-specific courses, and as a key assessment during practice in schools. Strong pre-service programs provide internship experiences in which pre-service teachers have the opportunity (and the responsibility) to interact with students and demonstrate their ability to effectively plan for diverse learners.

Again, when new teachers enter classrooms and must meet provisional licensure standards, knowledge of content and students is a consistent measure. The continuum of commitment follows the new teacher into his or her first job, as both new teacher induction programs and subsequent professional development standards provide opportunities for teachers to strengthen and share how they meet their responsibility to students. Follow-up of graduates by pre-service training institutions is essential to this process; such institutions need to determine where their graduates teach, whether they do a good job, how long they remain in the classroom, and so on. Professional development programs within schools have several roles to play, in mentoring new teachers who have been hired, but also in evaluating practicing teachers. In both cases, using the NBPTS core propositions as a framework can guide this work.

The continuum of professional development is enhanced by the obvious overlaps between the INTASC and NBPTS standards for teacher licensure. Emerging from the recent report *What Matters Most* (National Commission on Teaching and America's Future, 1996), are guidelines for reform of education that emphasize the integrated nature of the standards of national groups such as the INTASC, the NCATE, the NBPTS, and content standards groups, such as the NCTM, the NCTE, and the National Council for the Social Studies (NCSS). This report recommends a possible continuum of support to guide quality teacher preparation and development, a process that would begin with the recruitment and quality preparation of teacher candidates in fifth-year or graduate programs in teacher education—programs that meet the standards of NCATE. New teachers would be mentored by master teachers, using the INTASC induction standards; after three years in the classroom, teachers are eligible and could apply to become NBPTS certified, using the rigorous standards developed by the NBPTS. Primary to all standards is content knowledge. Throughout the entire process, the content standards for the various disciplines guide teacher knowledge as well as student achievement.

Integrating common beliefs about effective teacher practice into the continuum of teacher professional development strengthens the skills teachers need to continually monitor and assess the individual needs of the increasingly diverse population teachers currently face.

Promoting Teacher Leadership

Although research on the effects of NBPTS certification on student learning has just begun, our experience suggests that NBPTS certification is identifying teachers who are not only strong in the classroom, but who are also emerging leaders in education—both locally and nationally.

Teachers are the best informed persons about their own practice. National Board certified teachers (NBCTs) have demonstrated their knowledge, and in increasing numbers they are offering to share their expertise. They are essential and valuable partners. The process outlined in this book uses this collaborative approach. Facilitators cannot know all the answers. They guide and collaborate, but clearly do not direct; they are facilitators working with those who know students the best.

In addition to their work with colleagues who seek to demonstrate their classroom expertise, NBCTs are strong advocates for students and schools. They provide a presence at conferences, workshops, and roundtable discussions across the country where they provide a public voice that illustrates the strength of the teaching profession.

CREATING A COMMUNITY OF LEARNERS

There are several keys in this effort to create a continuum of education and demonstrate practice that can improve schools for all students:

- An understanding of the interrelationships of the various standards groups is essential.
- Openness to collaboration with like-minded groups is critical, whether they be from schools, government, business, or the community. Many groups have a stake in effective

schools that educate students well. They should be encouraged to play a role, but the goals and objectives should be set by educators.

- Work must be done with teachers, not directed at them. NBCTs are key players as planners and trainers.
- There must be recognition that real change takes time.

CONCLUSION

Change takes time. As Debra Meier (1995) noted in her description of the 15-year effort to build a more effective school for student learning at Central Park East in New York City, change is a slow process; real change in education is even slower. However, her results bear examination and emulation. There are many lessons to be learned from her experience, not the least of which is to recognize that collaboration by committed teachers and the time to allow an idea to develop can produce the kind of success she experienced in Harlem.

Most of the work in our development of the Collaborative Model of Support involved collaboration with teachers, with colleagues at associations, and with faculty at other colleges and universities. The goal, like that of our collaborators, is to produce strong schools with competent teachers who actively work to produce well-educated, well-prepared, lifelong learners.

To accelerate the climb toward such schools, we suggest:

- **To everyone interested in effective education for our children:** Get serious about standards for both students and teachers. They are not mutually exclusive, but rather are intimately connected. One will not happen without the other.
- **To schools, colleges, and universities:** Reinvent teacher preparation and professional development (Blackwell & Dietz, 1998; Browne, Auton, & Futrell, 1998). As we have mentioned throughout this book, the connection between pre-service teacher preparation (at the university) and in-school professional staff development is important for the success of all teachers. The links between INTASC, content standards, and NBPTS are intentional. They are all-important—together. Currently several universities around the country are involved in a collaboration to develop an advanced master's degree program whose focus is the ongoing education of teacher leaders.

    Improve recruitment of teacher candidates and be aware of the teaching abilities of those in your university classrooms. Are your faculty demonstrating the kind of teaching you would expect from P–12 teachers? This challenges universities to think carefully about the changing NCATE standards and the drive to improve the quality of both their programs and the potential teachers they recruit, as well as those who teach the discipline-specific courses in colleges of arts and sciences.
- **To businesses and legislatures:** Encourage and reward teacher knowledge and skill. This is a task beyond the competence at colleges and universities. It is made possible when teachers can prove that they are professional in their own practice and are the most skilled individuals to address the issues of diverse learners in varying subjects. Questions are always raised about what incentives exist for NBCTs. The NBPTS keeps a list that is updated biannually. Examples range from payment of the assessment fee to recertification credit to salary increases to local and state recognition. The incentives are initiated in local school systems, state legislatures, and universities.

- **To school districts:** Create schools that are focused on and organized for student and teacher success. According to a chart comparing educational staff by function (Organization for Economic Cooperation and Development, 1995, pp. 176–177, cited in National Commission on Teaching and America's Future, 1996, p. 19), the United States has the lowest percentage of teachers in relation to administrative staff in the industrialized world. In the United States, teachers make up about 32% of the total school staff, whereas in Denmark, our nearest competitor, almost 60% of the schools' total staff are teachers. Putting more trained adults in daily classroom contact with students multiplies the possibilities for successful schools. Professional teachers should argue that position to those who can make the changes.

Reform in education is dependent on teachers who are highly accomplished in their practice. The role of university/school facilitators and partners increases the likelihood that students will succeed. We believe that we have begun the process with the increasing prominence of the NBPTS and the further merging of other sets of standards that address various aspects of the teaching/learning process. It is a true community effort. This book has provided one model that can help to bring a community network together to improve the quality of teaching. We challenge you to join us in carrying it out.

RESOURCES

Argyris, C. (1992). *On organizational learning.* Cambridge, MA: Blackwell.

Blackwell, P., & Diez, M. (1998). *Toward a new vision of master's education for teachers using National Board standards and processes as benchmarks.* Washington, DC: National Council for Accreditation of Teacher Education.

Browne, B., Auton, S., & Futrell, M. (1998). *Creating partnerships to improve quality teaching: Reflections from a partnership.* Washington, DC: National Council for Accreditation of Teacher Education.

Council of Chief State School Officers. (1996). *Interstate school leaders licensure consortium: Standards for school leaders.* Washington, DC: Author.

Delpit, L. (1995). *Other people's children: Cultural conflict in the classroom.* New York: New Press.

Haycock, K. (1998). Good teaching matters . . . a lot. *Thinking K–16, 3*(2), 3–14.

Interstate New Teacher Assessment and Support Consortium. (1992). *Model standards for beginning teacher licensing and development: A resource for state dialogue.* Washington, DC: Council of Chief State School Officers.

Lambert, L., Collay, M., Dietz, M., Kent, K., & Richert, A. E. (1996). *Who will save our schools? Teachers as constructivist leaders.* Thousand Oaks, CA: Corwin Press.

Ladson-Billings, G. (1994). *The dreamkeepers: Successful teachers of African American children.* San Francisco: Jossey-Bass.

Meier, D. (1995). *The power of their ideas: Lessons for America from a small school in Harlem.* Boston: Beacon Press.

National Board for Professional Teaching Standards. (1999). *What every teacher should know: The National Board certification process 1999–2000.* Southfield, MI: Author.

National Commission on Teaching and America's Future. (1996). *What matters most: Teaching and America's future.* New York: Author.

Ravitch, D., & Finn, C. (1987). *What do our 17-years-olds know?: A report in the first national assessment of history and literature.* New York: Harper & Row.

Rigden, D. (1996, December). How teachers would change teacher education. *Education Week, 16*(15), 64, 48.

Rose, M. (1999, February). Reaching for excellence. *American Teacher, 83*(5), 6–7, 14.

Senge, P. M. (1990). *The fifth discipline: The art and practice of the learning organization.* New York: Doubleday.

Stallworth, J. (1998, February). Practicing what we teach. *Educational Leadership, 55*(5), 77–79.

Steeves, K. A. (1998). Working together to strengthen history teaching in secondary schools [On-line resource]. American Historical Association. (Available at: http://www.theaha.org/pubs/steeves.html)

Index